Linbert Spencer is a lifelong member of the Salvation Army, and was a member of the Archbishop's Commission on Urban Priority Areas, which produced *Faith in the City*. He works as a consultant to government and other organizations on the issues involved in building multi-ethnic organizations.

SPCK Ministry Series

SUPPORTING NEW MINISTERS IN THE LOCAL CHURCH: A HANDBOOK
Keith Lamdin and David Tilley

COMMUNITY AND MINISTRY: AN INTRODUCTION TO COMMUNITY DEVELOPMENT IN A CHRISTIAN CONTEXT
Paul Ballard and Lesley Husselbee

Wesley

BUILDING A MULTI-ETHNIC CHURCH

SPCK Library of Ministry

LINBERT SPENCER

SPCK

First published in Great Britain in 2007

Society for Promoting Christian Knowledge
36 Causton Street
London SW1P 4ST

British Library Cataloguing-in-Publication Data
A catalogue record for this book is available from the British Library

ISBN 978–0–281–05905–8

1 3 5 7 9 10 8 6 4 2

Typeset by Graphicraft Limited, Hong Kong
Printed in Great Britain by Ashford Colour Press

Produced on paper from sustainable forests

My thanks go to the very many individuals in the Salvation Army whose nurturing and support of me over many years have made this book possible, and to my family – especially my wife Marlene, eldest son Matthew and my mum – for their patience, belief in me and consistent support and encouragement. Saying thanks seems hardly adequate; but thank you all the same.

Contents

Preface

I was born in Jamaica in 1948 and was brought to England by my mother on a cold grey day in November 1955. Unlike my mother and I who had flown to England, my father had travelled by ship some six months earlier. On arrival he had been received by a friend who had already found him somewhere to live and a job with British Rail. After about six months he had saved enough money to send for me and my mother. Like many other Caribbeans in the 1950s my parents had decided to migrate because they wanted to secure a better future for me. They came to England because my father could not get a work permit to go to America, but Britain was asking the 'colonies' to send labour.

Our first home in England, which we lived in for a number of years, was one room in a boarding house in Harlesden, North West London. We shared the bathroom and kitchen with the five or six other families who lived in the house. My family were among the first Caribbeans or South Asians to settle in that part of London. During the following ten years we were witness to many changes in the complexion of the area.

Compared to many other migrants I think our introduction to, and integration into, life in Britain was relatively straightforward because of our membership of the Salvation Army. My parents had been member of the Salvation Army in Jamaica and had attended the Corps in Kingston. (At the time of writing, my 95-year-old mother is back in Jamaica and is still attending Kingston Central Salvation Army most Sunday mornings.) Because we belonged to this international Church, we simply transferred from one 'branch' which happened to be in Kingston, Jamaica, to another branch which happened to be in Harlesden, England. As a consequence we were welcomed as members and friends by our English Salvationist 'brothers and sisters'. In fact the transfer process of our paperwork was so smooth that at the time a number of Salvation Army Officers noted that the paperwork could not have been handled more smoothly if we had been coming from Kingston-on-Thames.

The reception into our church that my family experienced was not the norm. History shows that the majority of churchgoing Caribbeans who arrived in England during that time did not feel very welcomed at church, all be it that in the Caribbean they had attended a church belonging to the same denomination.

I lived in the London Borough of Brent for 17 years. The demographic changes between 1955 and 1972 were dramatic. During my time in Brent we moved from a situation where virtually all the families of Caribbean origin were known to each other to one where a significant proportion of the borough were of minority ethnic origin. Today more than 50 per cent of the population are of minority ethnic origin. Having said that, the 'White British' are still by far the largest single group in the borough.

A few years ago, I visited Furness Road Junior School, the first school I attended in England. It has a wonderfully multi-ethnic, multicultural mix of pupils and teachers. In November 1955, I was the only black or brown face to be seen.

Linbert Spencer

Introduction

It is a strange phenomenon in Britain, and I think in all the western democracies, that institutions, of whatever kind, find it almost impossible to respond positively to the idea that action is necessary if they are to include their minority ethnic communities and thereby begin to reap the potential benefits of ethnic diversity. The Church is, sad to say, no different in this respect, and in many ways it is just another Eurocentric institution.

The difficulty institutions have is one of failing to understand the difference between allowing people to participate, and actively seeking the participation of those who are not already participating. This difficulty is compounded by the oft-present phenomenon of institutional inertia. I don't believe that institutions ever consciously decide that they will never change; it's just that most people in organizations tend to get comfortable with the way things are. In church we're no different, whether it's the times of the service, the music that accompanies the singing, tea/coffee after the service (or not), the way the house groups are organized, how the Sunday school is run, not to mention who sits on which 'pew'. And so it goes on; we are generally more comfortable with the way things are, with what we have become used to, familiar with the familiar.

I suspect that although there is a general lack of awareness and understanding when it comes to the question of multi-ethnic church, institutional inertia is probably the most critical factor causing the Church not to be more responsive to the opportunity Britain's minority ethnic communities represent. Whatever the cause, I believe that if church leaders were to declare that they valued ethnic diversity, develop programmes of action to reach out to and attract minority ethnic Britons and teach and encourage all church members to recognize the value of ethnic diversity, then the Church would once again begin to grow in our cities.

The size of the Church in UK cities is now much smaller than it was in the 1950s. This decline has taken place alongside the increase of minority ethnic people in our cities. The economic migration from Bangladesh, India, Pakistan and the Caribbean, especially since the 1950s, and the more recent migration from Africa and Eastern Europe, has added to the rich mix of culture inherent in our cities. Our cities, often the drivers of wealth, are also places where there is great poverty and, in the midst of the hustle and bustle of the crowd, loneliness and isolation.

If the Church still sees itself as having a mission to the poor and the disenfranchised, then it cannot retreat from the cities. And if it is to be relevant in the cities, it cannot afford to be passive, but must be proactive when it comes to taking action to include Britain's minority ethnic communities.

Who should read this book?

This book should be read by church leaders – ordained and lay – and anyone involved in providing initial and in-service training for church leaders, ordinands and others in training.

The purpose of the book is to offer those involved in church leadership, information, advice and guidance regarding the Church and minority ethnic communities in Britain. The intention is to inspire them to be more proactive in providing the leadership necessary to enable the Church to more nearly reflect the ethnic diversity of the UK – to be the Kingdom now.

Throughout the book, references to Church or church leaders/leadership or leadership groups should be assumed to include General Secretaries, Principals, Directors and others in senior leadership roles within the relevant organizations.

This book can be used by individuals or in teams to:

- support individual growth and development
- support or deliver training
- enable leaders, stakeholders and the wider community to better understand the issues
- develop policy, strategy and implementation plans.

It can also be used by churches and other organizations working in partnership with each other.

Why it matters

- Combating discrimination, promoting equal opportunity and valuing diversity is biblically founded, morally right and socially desirable.
- A diversity of perception, thinking and approaches (all of which are more likely when a worshipping community is made up of people from different backgrounds) adds value to the fellowship because the worshipping community is enriched, its social endeavour strengthened and the values of the Kingdom of God are demonstrated.
- By increasing the involvement of minority ethnic members we will increase the quality, capacity and evangelical and service potential of our fellowship.

1

Biblical context

> Then Jesus came up and said to them, 'All authority in heaven and on earth has been given to me. Therefore, as you go, make disciples of all nations (not just believers), baptizing them in the name of the Father, and of the Son, and of the Holy Spirit, teaching them to obey all that I have commanded you. And remember, I am with you every day until the end of the age.' (Matt. 28.18–20)

I suspect that the command to go and make disciples of all nations was, and still is, a strong driver for overseas missions and missionaries. But we have 'all nations' here, just where we live and in the towns and cities in which we worship. This is a powerful command to create a multi-ethnic Church.

In his book *Intelligent Church*, making reference to the passage, Steve Chalke writes:

> The word *ethnos* which we have translated as 'nation' is more accurately translated 'ethnic-group' or even 'tribe'. In other words it defines people by their language, customs, beliefs, morals, values and culture rather than by their geography or country of residence. Jesus is calling His followers to take the issue of ethnicity and situation seriously and to work with it and respect it rather than be blind to it or attempt to ignore it. (p. 40)

> 'Of these three men, who do you think was a neighbour to the man who fell into the hands of the bandits?' He said, 'The one who showed mercy to him.' Jesus told him, 'Go and do what he did.' (Luke 10.36–37)

> But one of them, when he saw that he was healed, came back and praised God with a loud voice. He fell on his face at Jesus' feet and thanked him. Now the man was a Samaritan. Jesus asked, 'Ten men were made clean, weren't they? Where are the other nine?' (Luke 17.15–17)

> A Samaritan woman came to draw some water, and Jesus said to her, 'Please give me a drink.' For his disciples had gone off into town to buy food. The Samaritan woman said to him, 'How can you, a Jew, ask for a drink from me, a Samaritan woman?' For Jews do not have anything to do with Samaritans. (John 4.7–9)

In the time when Jesus walked this earth Samaritans were despised by the Jews and had been taught to hate the Jews. When it comes to us being guided as to who the gospel is for and where the boundaries for inclusion lie, the significance of these references cannot be overstated. In asking the Samaritan woman for a drink Jesus was enabling her to serve, to contribute, to add value. For those who belong to traditionally marginalized groups, the exclusion is not only experienced in terms of not being able to 'get', it is also experienced in not being able to 'give'. For Jews and Samaritans read any polarized countries or communities in conflict in our world today – Israel and Palestine, America and Iran. Your church and the kids on the corner?

> The Word became flesh and pitched his tent among us. We gazed on his glory, the kind of glory that belongs to the Father's only Son, full of grace and truth. (John 1.4)

So exactly what colour did this flesh become when it 'pitched his tent among us'? Jane Elliott, an outspoken and controversial White American equality consultant and trainer, says with reference to myriad images of Jesus in western Christian tradition, 'The real miracle of Christmas is that a white blue-eyed mother and her white blue-eyed baby Jesus were able to hide amongst swarthy brown-eyed Arabs.'

> 'All of these people who are speaking are Galileans, aren't they? So how is it that each one of us hears them speaking in his own native language? We are Parthians, Medes, Elamites, people from Mesopotamia, Judea, Cappadocia, Pontus, Asia, Phrygia, Pamphylia, Egypt, the district of Libya near Cyrene, and visitors from Rome. We are Jews, proselytes, Cretans, and Arabs. Yet we hear them telling in our own tongues the great deeds of God!'
> (Acts 2.7–11)

God is clearly into diversity and inclusion. The people were hearing the message in their own language and dialect, their diversity was being recognized and valued and they were all fully included in the good news of salvation. Diversity is not the enemy of inclusion and being included does not mean we all have to be the same.

In *Intelligent Church*, Steve Chalke writes:

> All those who had gathered in Jerusalem on that day could speak the same language. How do we know that? Because they were all Jews. Hebrew was the common language of the Jews, and Greek was the official language of the Eastern Roman Empire. So, two perfectly good global languages that the disciples were fluent in could have been used to communicate to the crowds that day. But God met the people using words that they learnt on their mother's knee – the words and phrases that they thought and dreamt in.
>
> Perhaps the greatest miracle of Pentecost is this: God chooses to speak to us in our own language. He is no one-size-fits-all policy. He comes to us. He begins where we are.
>
> If the incarnation is God personally involving Himself with His people, the day of Pentecost is God miraculously equipping the Church to do the same. This same task remains the challenge for the Church today: to start where people are, to engage in our communities, to embrace the public – in short, to speak their language. (p. 41)

> Now Barnabas, Simeon called Niger, Lucius from Cyrene, Manaen who had been brought up with Herod the tetrarch, and Saul were prophets and teachers in the church at Antioch.
>
> (Acts 13.1)

In *Dynamic Diversity*, Bruce Milne writes:

> The diversity of this Syrian congregation emerges in the description of the congregation's leadership team, five in number: Barnabas – from Cyprus; Simeon called Niger – 'the black', an African; Lucius of Cyrene – a North African; Manaen – possibly a slave of Herod's father, a Palestinian Jew; and Saul of Tarsus – a native of Asia Minor, the land bridge to Europe.

> Ray Bakke (*A Theology as Big as the City*) cites the archaeological evidence that the city, not unlike Jerusalem of our own time, was divided into distinct ethnic sectors, separated by walls, in this case five in number: Greek, Syrian, Jewish, Latin and African. Just as the coming of the gospel effectively destroyed the 'dividing wall of hostility' between Jew and Gentile, so it effectively destroyed the interior walls of Antioch to enable men, women and children from every sector to come together to hear the gospel and become followers of the 'Lord Jesus'.
>
> It is also highly significant that it was here that the name 'Christian' began to be applied to the followers of Jesus – a further critical indication of their sheer 'newness', but a newness, be it noted, expressed not least in the diversity of their community. Is it too much to claim that we truly justify our right to the name 'Christian' only when we practise diversity in unity under Christ? (p. 48)

> After these things I looked, and there was a large crowd that no one was able to count! They were from every nation, tribe, people, and language. (Rev. 7.9)

> In this new life one's nationality or race . . . is unimportant . . . whether a person has Christ is what matters, and he is equally available to all. (Col. 3.11)

Sadly for all of us, at least some of the time, colour, ethnic origin or nationality matters and it affects how we view and subsequently treat other people. In addressing this issue, our language does not always help us. When we use phrases like 'race relations', 'race equality' or 'racial justice' the implication is that people from different races need to get on better or do not get equal treatment, or people from a particular race are being treated unjustly. In fact, there is only one race – the human race. We must not allow the imperfections of our language to mislead us. 'So God created man in his own image . . . male and female created he them' (Gen. 1.27). I have been reflecting recently on what the image of God is, given that he created me in his own image. And if I am in his image, then in whose image are all those who do not look like me created?

In Matthew 22.38 (TLB) we are commanded to 'Love your neighbour as much as you love yourself' and it is made very clear in the parable of the good Samaritan (Luke 10.25–37) just who is our neighbour. However, not everyone gets neighbourly love. Visible minorities in the UK experience the injustice of racial discrimination through negative treatment and verbal abuse on a daily basis. It ranges from 'being invisible' and therefore ignored, to severe physical violence that results in fatal injuries. If the Church is to make a difference in the struggle to bring about the more just society implied in Colossians 3.11 we must attend to three Rs: recognition, repentance and reconciliation.

Recognition

'For the earth and every good thing in it belongs to the Lord and is yours to enjoy' (1 Cor. 10.26, TLB). The experience of many minority ethnic people in the UK is that this particular part of the earth is not theirs to enjoy, so much so, that we have anti-discrimination laws in the UK, a clear recognition that particular groups of people are treated sufficiently badly so as to require formal legal protection. The need for laws of this nature go right back to Old Testament times: 'Do not take advantage of foreigners in your land; do not wrong them. They must be treated like any other citizen; love them as yourself' (Lev. 19.33–34, TLB).

Recognition and acknowledgement of the negative treatment and abuse experienced by minority ethnic people in our society is a vital step if the Church through its individual members is to make a positive difference to all humankind enjoying the 'earth and every good thing'. Raise your awareness and increase your understanding by visiting minority ethnic community centres or talk to your local Community Relations Council or contact the relevant advisor at the national or regional offices of your denomination.

Repentance

'Let him who is without sin among you be the first to throw a stone at her' (John 8.7, RSV). We have doubtless all stereotyped people or made assumptions about individuals based on their colour, nationality or ethnic background, or because they were an asylum-seeker or refugee.

Reflection

- What do you think, believe or assume about refugees, asylum-seekers, Bangladeshi women, African men, Shiite Muslims?
- How did you come to these views?
- In the categories where you have a view, how many individuals have you actually met?

Most organizations in the UK, including the Church, have systematically failed to include and involve ethnic and cultural minorities at all levels of the organization. This failure is due to a number of things. One major reason is the beliefs many of us hold about the abilities, potential and commitments of ethnic and cultural minorities. We would do well to monitor how frequently we make assumptions and pre-judgements about people who are different from us.

> Get yourselves a new heart and a new spirit! (Ezek. 18.31, RSV)

> 'Repent, and be baptized every one of you in the name of Jesus Christ for the forgiveness of your sins; and you shall receive the gift of the Holy Spirit.' (Acts 2.38, RSV)

Reconciliation

Not only were we all created in God's image (Gen. 1.27), but in spite of our sin we have been reconciled to God through Jesus' death. 'We are no longer Jews or Greeks . . . we are all the same – we are one in Christ Jesus' (Gal. 3.28, TLB).

> 'If you enter your place of worship and, about to make an offering, you suddenly remember a grudge a friend has against you, abandon your offering, leave immediately, go to this friend and

> make things right. Then and only then, come back and work things out with God.' (Matt. 5.23–24, Message)

How much more important must it be for us to 'make things right' with minority ethnic people we stereotype or fail to see as equal because of their ethnic or cultural differences, or because when they demonstrate high levels of competence and ability we make them 'honorary whites', thus failing to acknowledge and celebrate their differences.

Jesus provides the ultimate model for individuals standing for racial justice. His example in asking the Samaritan woman for a drink (John 4.7–9) needs to be taken to heart.

2

Terminology and concepts

There is always a danger in overfocusing on terminology and what people or things are called. However, what we call things, and people, is often a reflection of how we see them and the value, values or abilities we ascribe to them. I think it is important therefore that we review and perhaps reflect on the meaning we give to and the assumptions we make when we use or hear the following words.

Asian

Asian is used to refer to people who are from, or descended from, Bangladesh, India or Pakistan; they do not necessarily see themselves as, or refer to themselves as, Asians. They would be more accurately described as South Asian. This distinguishes them from those originating from 'South East Asia' – e.g. Malaysia and Vietnam – and those originating from the North East Pacific Rim – e.g. Hong Kong and China.

Black

This is a term which can refer to any person of colour facing discrimination on the basis of skin colour, whatever their origin. This use of the term is intended to emphasize that all people facing such discrimination, whatever their differences, share that experience in common. It is a term of unity. Not everyone referred to by this usage of the term, however, chooses to use it in this way. Some people of African ancestry prefer 'African' to 'black'; many people of Asian ancestry prefer 'Asian' to 'black'. On the other hand, some people of light skin colour who experience discrimination on the basis of their ethnicity do choose to use the term 'black' to refer to themselves. In many parts of the voluntary and public sectors the terms 'Black and Asian' or 'Black and Minority Ethnic' are used as the inclusive terms for everyone who is not 'White British'.

Citizenship (see Nationality)

Most countries define citizenship in their constitutions. A country's constitution cannot be easily changed, nor is this done frequently. In the UK, where we do not have a constitution, ordinary legislation can change the definition of citizenship at any time, simply by the will of Parliament. In the last 50 years there have been a number of changes. For decades, the Home Secretary has had the power to deprive persons of British citizenship under limited conditions related to national security, but these powers have rarely been used. The person deprived must also have another nationality; the Home Secretary may not make a person stateless. Powers of deprivation were increased by legislation in 2002 and 2005. The present position is that a person may be deprived of British citizenship if the Home Secretary is satisfied that his or her citizenship is 'not conducive to the public good', or if naturalization was obtained by fraud or deception. The 'not conducive' condition is extremely vague; it appears to be chiefly concerned with terrorism, or incitement to terrorism, but it could be used much more widely. There is a limited right of appeal against deprivation. A person without nationality/citizenship of any state is stateless and has to depend for any rights on the laws of the particular state in which he or she is living. Since 1985 it has been possible for a child to be born stateless in the UK; a few hundred such children have however been registered annually as British after birth.

The UK remains liberal in its approach to including dual nationality, which many other states do not permit. So you can be a British citizen and have another nationality too, if your other state of nationality permits dual nationality. You cannot invoke the protection of one of your states of nationality when you are in the other state.

I was born in Jamaica in 1948 but my nationality was British. In 1962 when Jamaica gained independence I became a dual national Jamaican and British. In 1981 the British Nationality Act removed my British status and I became 'just' a Jamaican. In 1982, at a cost of £50, I purchased my British nationality by registration; thus becoming a British citizen and a dual national again.

Since 1 January 2004, all new applicants for British citizenship by naturalization or registration aged 18 or over have been required to attend a citizenship ceremony and take an oath and pledge of allegiance to the Queen and of loyalty to the United Kingdom's democratic values.

Culture

In the UN Covenant of 1966 on Economic, Social and Cultural Rights, culture was seen in terms of education and participation in cultural life – the arts and sciences. Everyone was to have the right of access to culture: books, theatre, dance and so on.

Archaeologists and anthropologists had their own definition of a culture as *the way of life* of a particular group. 'Neolithic culture', for example, meant the whole way of life, as far as it could be discovered, of New Stone Age people: their food, weapons, burial customs, building technology and so on. Applying a similar method, European and American anthropologists such as Bronislaw Malinowski and Margaret Mead made detailed studies of the ways people lived in the South Pacific and Africa, and gave accounts of religion, ritual, sexual behaviour and so on. Some of these accounts have since been heavily criticized by people from the 'cultures' that were studied. Nowadays, this anthropological meaning of culture has entered common usage. Generalizations about the 'cultures' of all sorts of groups, large and small, are made not just by scientific observers but by anyone at all. People may speak, for instance, of an office culture when describing the habits and conventions of those who work in offices. 'Consumer culture' and 'laddish culture' are accepted descriptions, and the Commission for Racial Equality's (CRE) formal investigation into the police forces of England and Wales makes reference to a 'canteen culture' in which expressions of racial prejudice and misogyny were common.

By far the most important place for culture in current social policy debates is in the attempt to reconcile the various 'cultures' of ethnic and religious minorities with that attributed to the tradition of the majority, with the purpose of defining a British culture that is, or ought to be, the property of all who live in Britain. When Asian, African and Caribbean immigrants became established in Britain in the 1960s, those who disliked them were sometimes unwilling to appear to object to their 'race' and protested that these people had a different culture: their cooking smelt funny; their clothes were odd; they did not fit in. For the most part, these particular objections have long since vanished, but insistence on the difference of cultures has persisted.

There is no necessary link between culture and immigration. By far the most important cultural influence on Britain in the last half-century has been that of the USA. Moreover, while some immigrant groups, such as those from the Indian subcontinent, have had a lot of cultural influence in the country as a whole, others have had very little except in limited localities. The commercial forces of globalization have been more influential than new settlement.

Of course, in the sense of culture as a set of attitudes, behaviour patterns and beliefs, there are indeed many different cultures in Britain, not least among the long-established population, where the differences may be defined by social class, region or dialect. It is important that these different cultures are known about and understood if people are to live peaceably together, and it is undeniable that problems can arise – for example, from varying attitudes to marriage. A problem with giving too much emphasis to the notion of culture, however, is that some people, especially in official circles, have come to expect that an individual's culture should be predictable because of his or her membership of a certain group. Both officials and journalists find it too easy to lump certain people together as a group and then assert what their 'culture' is.

culture is "the way we do things round here".

The definition that resonates most powerfully for me is that put forward by Charles Handy, writer, broadcaster and social philosopher: culture is 'the way we do things around here'. It is, at once, simple and profound.

Discrimination

In this context, discrimination is action or practices carried out by members of dominant groups or their representatives that has a differential and negative impact on members of a subordinate group. It is action that advantages some and disadvantages others, and unfair or unequal treatment which is usually, though not necessarily, based on prejudice. It is a way of acting that spoils other people's lives and life chances: when some minority ethnic groups get second-rate treatment in access to work, education or the provision of services, that is 'racial' discrimination.

Ethnicity

Ethnicity is the genetic inheritance that we have received from our ancestors and share with other members of our particular 'people group' – English, Indian, Irish, African-Caribbean etc.

While 'race' has no exact legal definition, the House of Lords has provided a definition of 'ethnic group' as a group that regards itself, or is regarded by others, as a distinct community by virtue of certain characteristics that will help to distinguish the group from the surrounding community. Two of these characteristics are essential:

- a long-shared history, of which the group is conscious, as distinguishing it from other groups, and the memory of which it keeps alive; and
- a cultural tradition of its own, including family and social customs and manners, often but not necessarily associated with religious observance.

Other relevant characteristics may (but need not) include common geographical origin or ancestry, a common language (not necessarily peculiar to the group), a common literature, a common religion and the status of either a minority or a dominant group within a larger community.

There are many difficulties of definition. Many Jews do not want to be defined as a racial or ethnic group. For the purposes of the Race Relations Act, however, they have been considered to be an ethnic group on the basis of their shared history – as have Sikhs, though Sikhism is a religion.

Each of us belongs to at least one ethnic group and may identify with several groups at the same time. (Someone could identify themselves as Yoruba or Nigerian or African or Black Briton.) In using the term 'minority ethnic group' in England, Wales, Scotland or Ireland we implicitly acknowledge that there is also a 'majority ethnic group' in each country.

Heritage (see also Culture)

'Heritage' is a term with a definite meaning: what is inherited, from people in the past. But its meaning, though clear, is very broad. It can mean material wealth, debts or privileges, ideas, buildings, history and more – anything we have not created or acquired by ourselves, from scratch.

A heritage can be a mixed blessing, with good features and bad. Britain's imperial heritage, for example, can be interpreted either as a sign that Britain has had a destiny to rule others, or as historical baggage that still causes us problems, or as a factor that helps make possible the development of multiracial society in Britain. It may be a tale of oppression and exploitation or a list of benefits, or both. Thus a word that is not in itself vague can be used for whatever purposes one wants, and should be treated with caution.

In the context of 'equality', heritage is frequently used in conjunction with, or instead of and taken to be synonymous with, culture and/or ethnic background or origin.

Nationality (see Citizenship)

'Nationality', in the sense of citizenship, is a legal status, acquired by birth or naturalization, that signifies which country one belongs to. A passport is issued on the basis of this legal status.

You may, for instance, be of Chinese ancestry but born or naturalized in France; you would then be a French national. Your nationality may be changed when the boundaries of a state are changed (as, for example, when the former state of Czechoslovakia became the two separate states, the Czech Republic and Slovakia, in 1993); or through naturalization (the process by which a country may confer its nationality on an applicant who fulfils its selection criteria). This does not change you personally, but it changes your legal position: for example, it may change your entitlement to vote or to work or the conditions under which you can enter particular countries, including your country of residence.

In many countries, nationality is the same as citizenship, but in Britain the situation is highly complicated. In law there are six categories of British national:

- British citizens
- British overseas territories citizens
- British overseas citizens
- British protected persons
- British subjects
- British overseas nationals.

British citizens are the only group with right of entry and abode in the UK. The others are all subject to immigration control, like aliens. These other groups are now quite small, and consist almost entirely of people of colour. It should be noted that the term 'British subject' now applies legally only to a few thousand people, mainly of Indian origin, but it is still used by some people as though it were the name of British nationality generally. This can cause confusion.

Right of abode (the right to live permanently in the country) is the only right British citizens have in nationality law. For other rights they depend on many separate pieces of legislation.

'National origins' are not limited to 'nationality' in the legal sense of citizenship of a nation state. The Scottish Court of Session has defined 'national origins' as '. . . identifiable elements, both historically and geographically, which at least at some point in time reveal the existence of a nation'. The nation in question need not exist any longer (Czechoslovakia, for example), and indeed may never have existed as a nation state in the modern sense ('the Basque nation', for example, or 'the Iroquois nation').

Prejudice

This refers to beliefs and values that lead people to be biased for or against members of a particular group. Prejudice means prejudging. The term is usually used to refer to hostile views rather than positive ones. Prejudiced opinions, by definition, are not rooted in full knowledge, but in unexamined and frequently negative impressions or misrepresentations.

Race

The word 'race' once meant simply 'family'. Later, it was used more loosely for national groups such as the English or French or German race. In the nineteenth century, scientists took it over to describe the 'races of Man' – groups defined by their physical differences from one another, such as skin colour, hair type, body shape and so on.

Numerous theories were developed about these different races, but there was no unanimity about what the races were. Some scientists put all Europeans together into a category, others divided them into 'Nordic', 'Alpine' and 'Mediterranean' races, or 'Teutonic' and 'Latin' races, or called all white people 'Caucasian'. Each race was supposed to have a set of moral and intellectual qualities linked to physique. The theorists, all North Europeans, were agreed on, unsurprisingly, the superiority of North Europeans in intelligence and morality. All regarded 'race' as an important determinant of individual character.

These theories have long been discredited as unscientific and hopelessly wrong. Even though there is obviously massive variation in the physical characteristics of human beings, the degree of variation among individuals who share common geographic origins is as wide as the variation between individuals with different geographical origins. However, the influence of racial theories on politics, popular fiction and journalism lasted well into the twentieth century. They dominated South Africa's apartheid policies until 1990, as well as the racial segregation of the Southern states of the USA. They shaped US immigration policies up to the 1960s, with national quotas set to encourage British, Irish and German entry and to discourage Indians and Chinese. They were at the root of British colonialism up to the Second World War, with preferential treatment and self-government for the 'White' Dominions; and after that war they underlay British governments' immigration policies. The essential feature was that 'races' were placed in order, from superior to inferior. The ordering sometimes differed, and the characteristics assigned to each race varied, but broadly speaking Europeans and their descendants living in other countries came out top; 'Orientals' such as Indians, Chinese and Japanese were in the middle; and Africans and their descendants were at the bottom of the pile.

The nineteenth-century scientists whose theories led to such beliefs were not eccentrics; they were highly respected intellectuals and leading thinkers. They were not involved in fringe politics nor were they fanatical about 'getting rid of people who were different'. They were serious scientists, all of whom had influence in high places. However, their apparently 'objective', 'scientifically valid' theories fed popular prejudices. Racial discrimination is one major result.

Under the Race Relations Act 1976, racial discrimination arises when a person or group is treated less favourably than another in similar circumstances 'on racial grounds'. These are defined as colour, race (which is given no further definition in the Act), nationality (including citizenship), or ethnic or national origins. This wide definition was necessary because of the remarkable variety of unfair treatment; discrimination might be on the grounds that a person was black (colour), Chinese (ethnic or national origins rather than nationality if the person came from Malaysia), or Pakistani (nationality), and it included discrimination against white people (grounds of colour), or against Europeans of particular nationalities (for example, Germans).

The pseudo-scientific myths about race mentioned above were discredited by two important developments in the early twentieth century: the new science of genetics, and sociology. Perceptions have also been changed by political events, such as Japan's defeat of Russia in the war of 1905; movements for colonial freedom around the world, and revulsion against Nazi racism. After the Second World War, the newly formed United Nations Organization was active in promoting international agreements designed to overcome racial discrimination, and many publications have exploded old ideas about race. These ideas still linger in some quarters, but they have largely lost political respectability.

The biological differences between us are much less significant than the similarities. Theologically, all are equally created by God and are children of God. We recommend avoiding using the word to refer to particular groups of people instead of humanity as a whole.

Racism

This refers to action based on the belief that there are different 'races' within humanity and that some are superior to others. It consists of conduct, words or practices that disadvantage or benefit people because of their colour, culture or ethnic origin. Racism may be personal, unconscious and unintentional as well as overt and deliberate. It has particular force when manifested in the major structures and institutions of society, which create and maintain the power and influence of one ethnic group at the expense of others (see 'Institutional racism'). In its subtle forms it is as damaging as in its overt form.

Institutional racism

The Macpherson Report of the investigation into the murder of Stephen Lawrence defined this as:

> the collective failure of an organization to provide an appropriate and professional service to people because of their colour, culture, or ethnic origin. It can be seen or detected in processes, attitudes and behaviour which amount to discrimination through unwitting prejudice, ignorance, thoughtlessness and racist stereotyping which disadvantage minority ethnic people.

Such discrimination may also be deliberate.

Racial harassment

This is unwanted conduct that violates people's dignity or creates an intimidating, hostile, degrading, humiliating or offensive environment because of their nationality and ethnic or national origins. It is usually inflicted by people who believe that there are different 'races' and that some are better than others.

White

This term is based on skin colour and refers to the majority of the population of Britain and Ireland. Although white people are culturally and ethnically diverse, they are often seen, and may see themselves, as a group and as the 'norm'. Because of Europe's imperial history, their skin colour has frequently given white people a sense of superiority and has acted as a kind of 'passport' to unearned privilege and more favourable treatment. This does not mean that there are not more white people who are homeless or who suffer discrimination for other reasons than black or

Asian people; but it remains the case that British and Irish institutions, including the churches, have been and still are controlled by white people while others have found it more difficult to gain access to positions of influence within them.

3

Migration into the UK

Twentieth-century migration

Many of us working to encourage greater involvement of people of minority ethnic background in British society generally and the Church in particular are often asked questions like, 'Well, why are they here anyway?'

The following summary of twentieth-century migration into the UK might help you to fashion a more confident and helpful response to such a question in future. In this way you might create more allies and alliances to help with the creation of a more multi-ethnic Church.

1905: Aliens Act passed

This legislation, aimed at restricting Jewish immigration from Eastern Europe, prohibits entry to Britain by 'undesirable aliens'. This term encompasses 'paupers, lunatics, vagrants and prostitutes'.

1914: refugees from the First World War

At the outbreak of war, many thousands of Belgians take refuge in Britain, although most will return after 1918. Nearly 29,000 Austrians and Germans are instantly repatriated under the Aliens Restrictions Act. More than 32,000 other 'non-British' nationals are interned in prison camps, where they will remain for the course of the war. This legislation also created, for the first time, a clear definition of British nationality in law, and sets out how the police and the army should treat 'aliens'.

1916: Caribbeans aid war effort

Thousands of Caribbean people arrive in Britain's seaports and major cities to work in munitions factories, armouries and the merchant navy. They establish themselves in the seaports and major cities, where their presence leads to race riots in the years immediately following the First World War.

1917: Russians flee October Revolution

Small numbers of Russians, escaping the Bolshevik Revolution, establish a tight-knit community in London. Britain signs an agreement with Russia that men born in Russia, now living in Britain but not naturalized, would have either to serve in the British army or return to Russia and serve in the Russian army.

1920: passport stop lists introduced

Political activists with a history of anti-British activity in India are refused entry to Britain.

1925: new law targets black seamen

The Special Restriction (Coloured Alien Seamen) Order makes it compulsory for all 'coloured alien seamen' to register with the local police within a limited number of days. Initially, Yemeni seamen are the main target, and the law is actively enforced in only a small number of ports. But within a year the order is applied to all British ports and to all 'coloured' sailors, effectively amounting to a 'colour bar' on work at sea.

1938: Jews flee from Nazi persecution

With the National Socialist Party in Germany pursuing an ever more vigorous campaign of persecution against the Jews, nearly 10,000 unaccompanied Jewish children arrive in Britain from Germany, Austria and Czechoslovakia via the Kindertransport programme.

1940: foreign pilots in the Battle of Britain

Britain faces an urgent need for fighter pilots as it becomes clear that Hitler would attempt to defeat her with air power. Trained pilots from the Caribbean, South Africa, India and Eastern Europe (especially Poland and Czechoslovakia) join the fighter squadrons and play a major part in repulsing the Luftwaffe. Some squadrons are made up entirely of South Africans or Poles. After the Battle of Britain is won, many of these migrant pilots go on to serve in the bomber squadrons of the Fleet Air Arm.

1941: migrant labour helps sustain war effort

During the Second World War, more than 60,000 Irish men and women work in Britain, manufacturing munitions, equipment and food supplies for the war effort, and helping to fill the gaps left in public services.

1946: rebuilding post-war Britain

Displaced people living in refugee camps all over Europe take advantage of various resettlement schemes, such as the European Volunteer Workers scheme. For example, 85,000 Ukrainians, Yugoslavs, Estonians, Latvians and Lithuanians come to Britain between 1946 and 1950, while 100,000 Polish refugees who did not want to return to communist Poland decide to stay in Britain. Some 15,700 German and 1,000 Italian POWs remain in Britain after the war.

Around 345,000 Germans, Italians, Ukrainians, Austrians and Poles were recruited through work-permit schemes and, by 1952, 110,000 have been resident in the country for over four years.

After the war, active recruitment also begins in Ireland, the Caribbean and the Indian subcontinent. By the end of the 1960s, there are 900,000 Irish-born immigrants in Britain, and about 1 million visible minorities.

1947: Australia incentivizes British émigrés

The Australian Government introduces the UK Assisted Passage Scheme, offering passages for £10 per adult and £5 for 14–18-year-olds. This would be followed in 1957 by the 'bring out a Briton' campaign, with the result that between 1961 and 1971 only 10 per cent of UK immigrants would be unassisted.

1947: partition in India

Britain relinquishes its rule over the Indian subcontinent, leaving it partitioned into two countries: mainly Hindu India, and a largely Muslim Pakistan. The next 25 years will see large numbers of people migrating to Britain from the subcontinent, mainly from Gujarat and the Punjab in India, Mirpur in Azad Kashmir (Pakistan), and Sylhet in Bangladesh (which, prior to its independence in 1971, was known as East Pakistan). By 1955, the total number of Indians and Pakistanis in Britain will reach 10,700.

With the newly established NHS in short supply of qualified doctors and nurses, the door is opened to medical professionals from other countries, so that by 1975, 84 per cent of junior medical hospital staff in geriatric care will come from overseas. However, most immigrants from the subcontinent come to fill unskilled jobs in the manufacturing sector, particularly in metalworking and textiles.

1948: the SS *Empire Windrush* docks in London

On 22 June, the SS *Empire Windrush*, carrying 450 Jamaicans (mostly ex-servicemen), docks at Tilbury, and receives an official welcome from the Government. This marks the beginning of a sustained period of migration from the Caribbean to Britain. Between 1955 and 1962, more than 250,000 people arrive in the UK from the Caribbean – predominantly Jamaica, including me. In 1961, the final year before Britain's first immigration law took effect, more than 66,000 make the journey.

1948: British Nationality Act introduced

British passport-holders are designated as citizens of 'the United Kingdom and Colonies'. This means every Commonwealth citizen is also a British subject, with the right of entry to the UK.

1951: arrivals from Italy

As part of Britain's rebuilding efforts following the end of the Second World War, men and women from the south of Italy are recruited to work in factories in Luton and Bedford. More than 7,000 went to work for just one firm – Bedford's Marston Valley Brick Company, which needed extra labour to meet the demands of the post-war reconstruction boom. Others went on to open Italian restaurants, pizzerias and other businesses.

1951: the UK signs the Refugee Convention

The United Nations Convention Relating to the Status of Refugees (the 'Refugee Convention') is signed by the British Government.

The Refugee Convention defines as a refugee anyone who (a) has a well-founded fear of persecution for reasons of race, religion, nationality, membership of a particular social group, or political opinion, (b) is outside the country they belong to or normally reside in, and (c) is unable or unwilling to return home for fear of persecution.

1952: US clampdown on Caribbean migrants

The US Government passes more stringent immigration legislation, making it more difficult for Caribbean migrants to gain entry. Many, including my parents, turn instead to Britain, which still has a relatively relaxed admissions policy.

1952: affordable air travel

In May, the first civilian jet airliner, the DeHavilland Comet, enters service in Britain. Its first scheduled flights are between London and Johannesburg. Although for the first few years air travel would remain the preserve of the rich, the cost soon fell, and this, combined with a rapidly increasing number of transcontinental routes, had a dramatic effect on migration throughout the world. It became easier to visit relatives 'back home', for example, and short-term migration (such as studying or taking up short-term work in other countries) became a more realistic option than before.

1957: European Economic Community established

Belgium, France, Italy, Luxembourg, the Netherlands and West Germany, known informally as the Common Market, sign a treaty in Rome establishing the EEC on 25 March.

1958: increasing public resistance to new migrants

White youths attack black people and businesses in Notting Hill and other areas of West London. The Government finds itself under increasing pressure to control immigration.

1962: Britain's first immigration legislation

The Commonwealth Immigrants Bill becomes law, removing the automatic right of Commonwealth citizens to gain entry to Britain (see 1948 above). From now on, the only people allowed to enter are holders of employment vouchers issued by the Ministry of Labour, students, members of the armed forces and entrants who can demonstrate their ability to support themselves and their dependants without working. Also, people registering for citizenship now have to demonstrate that they have resided in the UK for a certain period of time. The initial response to the Act is a tremendous drop in the number of Caribbean migrants entering Britain. Between 1955 and 1962, a quarter of a million had arrived from the Caribbean alone. Migration from South Asia, which had increased during the late 1950s to almost match the numbers of Caribbean migrants by 1961, is similarly affected.

During the period between 1955 and 1962 the rate of arrivals from the Caribbean and South Asia tracked, almost precisely, the rate of notified job vacancies. Prior to the 1962 Act, immigration from the 'new commonwealth' had been controlled economically. The advent of the 1962 Act destroys the relationship between arrivals and notified job vacancies.

1968: 'Rivers of Blood' and a new Immigration Act

The Kenyan Government bars foreigners from work, and thousands of Kenyan Asians who have British passports begin arriving in Britain at the rate of 1,000 per month. The Conservative MP Enoch Powell wins popular support for his anti-immigration 'Rivers of Blood' speech, and calls for the forced return of immigrants settled in Britain.

The Labour Government responds by rushing through a new Commonwealth Immigrants Act, which requires immigrants to demonstrate a 'close connection' with the UK. The Act also draws an important distinction between citizens who were 'patrials' – those who possessed identifiable ancestors in the British Isles – and those who were not. In practice, these 'patrials' were almost exclusively white. The practical effect of this is that people from the 'Old Commonwealth' – Australia, Canada, New Zealand and South Africa – were allowed to settle in Britain, if they chose to, while most potential migrants from South Asia and the Caribbean – 'new Commonwealth' – were not.

1971: Immigration Act 1971

This legislation introduces powers for immigration officers to detain asylum-seekers in immigration detention centres, or even prisons, while the Home Office considers their application.

1972: Asians forced out of Africa

Britain admits 28,000 Asians expelled from Uganda by its dictator Idi Amin. Many settle in Wembley in Middlesex (now the London Borough of Brent) and Leicester in the Midlands. Large numbers also arrive from Kenya, due to the Kenyan Government's 1968 legislation banning foreigners from working in the country.

The Government had initially been reluctant to admit the refugees, even though the majority were highly skilled and had British passports. They feared that they might destabilize race relations in the country, which had been increasingly strained since the mid-1960s.

1973: Britain joins European Economic Community

Britain enters the European Economic Community (later to become the EU), eventually paving the way towards economic and social integration more than two decades later (see 1957).

1974: Turkish invasion of Cyprus brings refugees to Britain

President Archbishop Makarios is briefly deposed in a military coup by Greek Cypriots seeking unification with Greece. Fearing for the rights of the minority Turkish population, Turkey invades northern Cyprus and expels Greek residents. The island is officially divided and the buffer zone between the two sectors is still patrolled by the UN more than three decades later. An estimated 20,000 Greek Cypriots flee the island and make their way to Britain.

1975: Britain votes to stay in EEC

The first national referendum ever held in Britain results in victory for the Labour Government's campaign to stay in the EEC. Just over 67 per cent of voters vote 'Yes' in response to the question, 'Do you think the UK should stay in the European Community (Common Market)?' The campaign succeeds despite several cabinet ministers having come out in favour of British withdrawal.

1975: first Vietnamese refugees arrive

The long-running war in Vietnam ends on 30 April when the Saigon Government announces its unconditional surrender to North Vietnamese forces. On 3 December 1977, the first boat people, as they become known, flee the now-communist Vietnam. Between 1979 and 1982, 12,500 refugees will arrive in the UK, many with little or no education and unable to write in their own language, let alone English.

1981: The Nationality Act (see 1948 and 1962)

The Conservative Government passes a new Nationality Act, which effectively removes the right to British citizenship from significant numbers of people from 'new Commonwealth' nations (in other words, those from the Caribbean, Bangladesh, India and Pakistan) who have previously been classed as British citizens.

In addition, Hong Kong British passport-holders were now no longer entitled to move to, and live in, the UK.

In 1992 the net inflow would increase to 240,000; and between 1993 and 2002 it would reach just over 1 million.

1981: Britain becomes net importer of people

For the first time in its history, the UK begins a sustained period where the number of people arriving in the country exceeds the number of those leaving it.

1986: immigration under strict control

As a result of the tighter immigration controls introduced during the 1980s, the bulk of new immigrants entering Britain are North Americans, Australians, New Zealanders and South Africans making use of family-ties entry rules – basically white people, and South Asian men and women entering the medical professions.

Between 1984 and 1986, only 240 applications for asylum were accepted for every 1 million of the UK's inhabitants, representing less than 0.1 per cent of the population. By comparison, Sweden takes 5,000 asylum-seekers per 1 million of its population, and Denmark and Switzerland more than 4,000 each (see 1951).

1987: Single European Act introduced

This Act, signed in the previous year by the 12 member states, is the first major amendment of the 1957 Treaty of Rome, which established the European Economic Community. It comes into force on 1 July 1987. The Act's main objective is to progressively establish a single internal market by 31 December 1992, that is, 'an area without internal frontiers in which the free movement of goods, persons, services and capital is ensured in accordance with the provisions of this Treaty'.

1989: collapse of communist regimes in Eastern Europe

Six communist governments in Eastern Europe are overthrown in a series of largely peaceful revolutions. The first to fall is in

Poland, followed by East Germany, Czechoslovakia, Hungary and Bulgaria. In Romania, the regime is overthrown by force and its head of state executed. The Baltic states of Lithuania, Estonia and Latvia declare independence from the Soviet Union shortly afterwards. This paves the way, in most cases, for open and fair multi-party parliamentary elections, and the enshrinement of human and civil rights in national constitutions.

1990: first Somali refugees arrive

The ousting of Somalia's Government in 1991 leads to prolonged civil war and tens of thousands of people fleeing the country. Many more Somalis leave in later years to escape severe famine that follows. The combined effect of these factors will see annual applications from Somalis for asylum in the UK rise from less than 400 in 1988 to 7,000 by 1999.

1991: Maastricht Treaty brings European integration closer

The Treaty promotes closer economic and political union through the establishment of a European currency and central bank, and harmonization of defence, foreign and social policies. It results in the transformation of the EEC into the European Union (EU) the following year.

1992: UK asylum applications plummet

The number of asylum applications halves in 1992 compared to the previous year. One significant factor in this is thought to be the Conservative Government's decision the previous year to double the carriers' liability fine. This had introduced increased penalties on airline or shipping companies who allowed people to board without a full set of travel documents. Critics of this legislation argue that thousands of refugees were prevented from fleeing persecution or death as a result.

1993: Asylum and Immigration Appeals Act

This new Act recognizes the right to asylum, but also gives the Home Office new powers to deport asylum-seekers within days of their arrival – and without a hearing – if it could be shown that, before arriving in Britain, they had stopped in a 'third country' where they could have applied for asylum instead.

A total of 10,530 people were detained this year under the new Act – twice the number for 1992.

1997: Primary Purpose Rule abolished

The newly elected Labour Government abolishes this rule, which required a British national who married a spouse from overseas to prove that the primary purpose of the marriage was not to settle in the UK.

1998: Kosovan Albanians flee civil war in Yugoslavia

More than 8,000 ethnic Albanians from Kosova arrive in Britain, many of them young single men in fear of their lives due to the continuing civil war in Yugoslavia. Most are granted temporary asylum, but nearly 600 are allowed to settle permanently.

2000: arrivals from Iraq, Afghanistan and Zimbabwe

The legacy of wars fought during the 1980s and 1990s in Iraq and Afghanistan bring asylum-seekers and refugees to Britain. In Zimbabwe, many white farmers (and British passport-holders) are persecuted by Robert Mugabe's Zanu-PF party and have their land rights confiscated, prompting many to leave the country for good.

2001: non-EU European migration

The Office for National Statistics reports that 46,000 people moved to the UK this year from non-EU Europe – that is, the former Eastern Bloc states, plus countries such as Turkey. It also estimates net total immigration from all countries to the UK at around 150,000 per year.

2001: census figures reveal extent of new migration

The 2001 census shows a 50 per cent increase in the size of the minority ethnic population compared with the figures from

1991. One in nine people are of minority ethnic origin – in other words, belonging to a group other than White British. The largest minority ethnic group in Britain – people of Indian descent – now numbers over 1 million, or just under 2 per cent of the population. The next largest groups were Pakistani (746,000), Irish (691,000), Black Caribbean (566,000) and Black African (485,000).

The total UK population increased by 2.2 million compared to 1991, some 1.14 million of whom were born abroad.

2002: record number of asylum requests

UN figures show that 103,000 people (24 per cent of the EU total) have sought asylum in the UK this year. This is the highest figure in the EU; Germany is next on the list with 17 per cent. The most common countries of origin for asylum-claimants during this year were Iraq, Zimbabwe, Afghanistan, Somalia and China. The Home Office later estimates that 42 per cent of applications resulted in grants of asylum.

2002: Highly Skilled Migrant Programme

The Government introduces the Highly Skilled Migrant Programme. This is a points-based system which allows migrants possessing certain skills to enter the UK and work without first having to find an offer of employment or having their visa application sponsored by an employer.

2003: Somalis top asylum list

According to the Home Office, the largest number of asylum applications came from nationals of Somalia (over 10 per cent of applications), Iraq (8 per cent), Zimbabwe (7 per cent), Iran (6 per cent) and Afghanistan (5 per cent).

2004: Workers' Registration Scheme

The Government brings in legislation requiring that workers register upon entering the country – the Workers' Registration Scheme (WRS). Most nationals of the new EU member states (except Cyprus and Malta) who want to work for more than one month for an employer in the UK need to register under the scheme. Those who have worked for at least 12 months in the UK no longer have to register on the scheme, and are entitled to a residence permit confirming their right to live and work in the UK.

During the first 18 months of the scheme, 293,000 immigrants apply for work permits. The majority are Poles (56 per cent), with the remainder made up of Lithuanians (17 per cent), Slovaks (10 per cent), Latvians, Czechs, Hungarians and Estonians (all under 10 per cent).

2004: EU expansion

On 1 May, nationals of the ten new countries admitted to the EU (including the Czech Republic, Slovakia, Estonia, Hungary, Latvia, Lithuania and Poland) obtain the right to travel freely and live anywhere in the enlarged EU. However, for up to seven years, the established fifteen member states may restrict the right to work of people from the eight Central and Eastern European accession countries. The UK, Ireland and Sweden are the only countries to open their labour markets to workers from these countries straightaway.

More people than the Government expected – around 130,000 – arrive in Britain as a result, representing the largest wave of immigration since the 1950s and 1960s.

2005: record migration pushes UK population beyond 60 million

Estimates from the Office for National Statistics suggest that nearly a quarter of a million more people entered the UK than left it between June 2004 and June 2005. This net increase of 235,000 was the largest yearly total since the current system of estimates began in 1991.

Migration into the UK was around 59,000 more than in the previous mid-year period, a rise of 11 per cent, and migration from the UK fell by 8,000.

2005: number of asylum-claimants reaches 13-year low

During the year, a total of 30,500 people seek refuge in the UK, according to figures published by UNHCR, the UN's refugee agency. This represents a 70 per cent drop compared to the record figures in 2002, and is the lowest total since 1993. The figures also reveal that the UK was the eighteenth most popular destination out of 50 industrialized nations, with 0.5 asylum applications per 1,000 people. This compared with 0.8 in France and 0.2 in the USA.

Iranians formed the largest group of people claiming asylum in the UK (3,990), followed by Somalis (3,295) and Pakistanis (3,030).

2005: 'illegal immigrant' controversy in election year

The Home Office puts the number of illegal immigrants in the UK at between 310,000 and 570,000.

However, other estimates, such as those released by the think-tank Migration Watch, suggest that the actual number is much higher – as many as 750,000 – prompting renewed public debate during election year about Britain's immigration and asylum policy.

2005: BBC publishes 'Born Abroad' database

The BBC publishes its 'Born Abroad' database, based on analysis carried out by the Institute for Public Policy Research on census 2001 figures. It reveals that 7.5 per cent of people living in Britain in 2001 were born abroad, representing 4.3 million people out of a total of 57 million.

2006: Eastern European workers head UK's 'biggest wave of immigration'

Home Office figures reveal that around 375,000 people from Eastern Europe have come to work in the UK since 2004 and the number of foreign workers in the UK now stands at 1.5 million, or 1 in every 25 workers.

Six out of every ten of these new migrants is Polish. Many are skilled and will find work in construction, agriculture, catering, retail and healthcare. Most have stayed in the south of England, with 34,000 living and working in London and 27,000 in East Anglia. More than 10,000 head for Scotland, where the Scottish Executive actively encourages immigration from the new EU countries as part of its Fresh Talent initiative.

4

Minority ethnic communities in the UK

Minority ethnic communities are defined as those communities that are not the 'majority ethnic community' and the majority ethnic community is made up of the people who tick the White British box on the national census form. At the last census (2001) the majority ethnic population totalled 50,366,497 – 88 per cent. This chapter provides a brief profile of Britain's minority ethnic communities.

The Black Caribbean group

Total population in Britain: 566,000
Proportion of all people in Britain: 1 per cent

Source: Census 2001, Office for National Statistics; Census 2001, General Register Office for Scotland

For the most part the Black Caribbean population is descended from people whose ancestors in the eighteenth century were taken as slaves from West Africa to British colonies in the West Indies. By the nineteenth century when slavery was abolished many British cities had small black populations. Today the main country of birth for the Black Caribbean population is England (57 per cent) and Jamaica (23 per cent), with 3 per cent born in Barbados and roughly 2 per cent each from Trinidad, Tobago, Guyana, Grenada, and smaller proportions born in a number of other countries, including countries outside the Commonwealth, such as Puerto Rico, the Dominican Republic and Cuba.

After the Second World War a number of Caribbean men who had served in the armed forces stayed in Britain, and in 1948 the

SS *Empire Windrush* brought a historic group of Jamaican immigrants to Tilbury (see page 23). Large-scale migration from the Caribbean only started in the 1950s after immigration to the USA became more difficult. By 1951 there were about 17,000 people born in the Caribbean living in Britain.

The majority of the Black Caribbean population live in London (61 per cent), with a further 15 per cent living in the West Midlands. The remainder are fairly evenly distributed among the other regions.

Age and sex profile

Early migrants from the Caribbean tended to come to Britain as family units, unlike those from South Asian countries. This contributed to the unique shape of the population pyramid for the Black Caribbean population which has three distinct peaks at around ages 60, 38 and 16. The first of these peaks represents the *Windrush* generation, most of the second generation and almost all of the third generation were born in Britain.

Unusually the Black Caribbean population has a greater number of women than men in the working-age population (54 per cent), which could be the consequence of an undercount of men. Uniquely more Black Caribbean females of working age are likely to be in professional or managerial occupational groups (30 per cent compared with 20 per cent). In all other groups the number of men and women is similar or men are the majority in this occupational group.

Religions

The Black Caribbean population has a similar religious profile to the While British population, with 74 per cent identifying themselves as Christian and 11 per cent with no religion. The Black Caribbean Christian population in Britain has tended to establish its own churches rather than joining the main denominations in the UK. Black Caribbeans have many other religious affiliations, including Islam, Rastafarianism and Jehovah's Witnesses.

Languages

Unlike most minority ethnic groups, foreign-born members of the Black Caribbean population tend to speak English as their first language.

The Black African group

Total population in Britain: 485,000
Proportion of all people in Britain: 0.8 per cent

Source: Census 2001, Office for National Statistics; Census 2001, General Register Office for Scotland

The Black African grouping is one of the most diverse in terms of country of origin and place of birth, with 34 per cent born in the UK, 16 per cent in Nigeria, 10 per cent in Ghana, 8 per cent in Ghana, 4 per cent in Zimbabwe, 3 per cent in Uganda and 21 per cent in other African states.

Patterns of migration

There has been a long history of small-scale migration from Sub-Saharan African nations with Somali sailors settling in Britain in the late nineteenth century and Black African communities forming in the major British seaports. Unsurprisingly in such a heterogeneous group, there were a range of factors driving migration. In the post-independence period the number of people travelling to Britain for education and technical training increased as the demand for skills and education could not be met locally. This continues to be a driving force in migration today, but economic pressures and political persecution also drive people to travel to Britain. From the 1960s onwards, political instability in various African nations including Kenya, Uganda and Malawi has contributed to increased migration to Britain. More recent conflicts such as those in Rwanda, Sudan and the Democratic Republic of Congo have also led to migration from Africa.

The Black African population in Britain is largely concentrated in London (78 per cent). The 2001 census shows that for the first time the Black African population in London outnumbers the Black Caribbean. There are also Black African communities in Liverpool, Leeds and Cardiff, historically centres of African migration.

Religions

According to the 2001 census, 69 per cent of Black Africans are Christian and 20 per cent Muslim. Only 2 per cent identified themselves as having no religion.

Age and sex profile

The median age of the Black African population is 27 for men and 28 for women, and 68 per cent are of working age. Slightly more women than men are in the working-age population (53 per cent), but among the over 65s, 52 per cent are male.

Languages

A multitude of languages are spoken by the Black African population. The more commonly spoken African languages include Swahili, Somali, Yoruba and Twi.

The Other Black group

Total population in Britain: 96,000
Proportion of all people in Britain: 0.2 per cent

Source: Census 2001, Office for National Statistics; Census 2001, General Register Office for Scotland

Of people identifying themselves as Other Black in the 2001 census, 79 per cent were born in Britain, 9 per cent were born in Africa, 5 per cent were born in the Caribbean, the remaining 7 per cent were largely from South and North America, with a small number born in the rest of the world. The majority identified themselves in the write-in box as having a Black British ethnicity.

Age and sex profile

With regard to the age and gender profile of the Other Black group, the majority were of working age (59 per cent) and most of the remainder (38 per cent) were under 16, with only 3 per cent aged 65 and older. The majority of people in this group were born in Africa (84 per cent of those of African origin) and the Caribbean (70 per cent) and were aged between 16 and 65. This is likely to be because of the large number of economic migrants in this group. Other Black Africans were most likely to be in the highest socio-economic group. Working-age men born in Africa were also least likely to be unemployed. The UK-born Other Black population had fewer people of working age (54 per cent) and the largest proportion under 16 (45 per cent). The oldest age profile was among those born in the Caribbean, of whom 25 per cent were over 65 – similar to the profile of the Black Caribbean population which has a distinctive peak above age 60, reflecting migration patterns.

Religions

The religious make-up of the Other Black population is largely Christian (67 per cent), with 12 per cent stating that they had no religion, 15 per cent opting not to state their religion and 6 per cent identifying themselves as Muslim. Christians accounted for the same proportion of people in the Other Black group born in the UK and Caribbean and the West Indies (69 per cent), but made up only 57 per cent of those born in Africa. A far larger proportion of Other Blacks born in Africa were Muslim (28 per cent), compared with those born in the UK (1 per cent) and the Caribbean and the West Indies (1 per cent).

The Chinese group

Total population in Britain: 243,000
Proportion of all people in Britain: 0.4 per cent

Source: Census 2001, Office for National Statistics; Census 2001, General Register Office for Scotland

In the national census the Chinese census group encompasses a number of Asian nations and there is no dominant country of birth. The proportions of the Chinese population born in the UK and in Hong Kong are the same (29 per cent), with 19 per cent born in China and 8 per cent in Malaysia. Smaller proportions of people were also born in Vietnam (4 per cent), Singapore (3 per cent) and Taiwan (2 per cent).

Patterns of migration

There has been immigration from mainland China to Britain since the nineteenth century, when sailors drafted into shipping firms such as the East India Company began to settle in Britain's larger ports. In the docks of East London, Liverpool, Bristol and Cardiff, Chinese laundries, lodging houses and restaurants were set up to cater for Chinese seamen ashore. The decline of the shipping industry in the 1930s saw some return to China, but the 1950s marked the beginning of a major wave of migration from Hong Kong, Singapore and Malaysia. Two decades of economic boom made Britain an attractive place to travel to for education and employment, especially for people living in the New Territories in Hong Kong, who were free to enter Britain and whose rice-based economy was suffering from the competition of cheap rice from Thailand and Burma. Many were single men with little intention of settling permanently who only brought their families over when it was clear that they would be staying. Since the 1980s there has been a new wave of migration from mainland China, largely in the form of people seeking educational opportunities. This is reflected in the large young Chinese population in the university towns of Oxford and Cambridge (2,460 and 2,325 respectively).

The Chinese population is most concentrated in London and the South East (33 per cent and 14 per cent respectively) with the rest spread fairly evenly around Britain. The relatively scattered distribution of this group partly reflects the fact that a high proportion of mid-twentieth-century migrants from Hong Kong set up restaurants and takeaways in places were there was little competition. As a result the 'Chinatowns' in British cities are small commercial districts rather than the larger residential neighbourhoods typical of the USA or Canada.

Religions

Of all the ethnic groups, the Chinese has the highest proportion of members with no religion (53 per cent). Of the remainder, 21 per cent identified themselves as Christian and 15 per cent as Buddhist – 25 per cent of the Buddhist population in Britain (White British people made up 34 per cent).

Age profile

The median age of the Chinese population is 27, with 76 per cent aged between 16 and 65, 19 per cent under 16, and 5 per cent over 65. The age profile of the Chinese population reflects the pattern of immigration to the UK, with a narrow base and a peak at about age 20, reflecting educational migrants from mainland China and a slow tapering at an older age reflecting the economic migrants from the 1950s and 1960s.

Languages

A range of Chinese dialects are spoken in Britain. Chinese migrants from Hong Kong and some parts of Southern China are likely to speak Cantonese and sometimes Hakka, whereas student migrants from mainland China tend to speak Mandarin, the official language of mainland China.

The 'Other' ethnic group

Total population in Britain: 229,352
Proportion of all people in Britain: 0.4 per cent

Source: Census 2001, Office for National Statistics; Census 2001, General Register Office for Scotland

The majority of people who identified themselves as the Other ethnic group were born in the North East Pacific Rim (53 per cent), more specifically the Philippines (15 per cent), Japan (15 per cent),

Thailand (5 per cent) and Vietnam (5 per cent). The second most common country of birth was the UK (16 per cent), with 10 per cent from the Middle East, including Iraq and Iran (3 per cent each). A further 7 per cent were born in an African country, including Egypt (2 per cent) and Morocco (1 per cent), and 6 per cent were born in a South Asian country, the majority of these in Afghanistan (5 per cent).

London is home to the largest proportion of people belonging to the Other ethnic group, with significant concentrations in the West Midlands, the East, the South East and the North West.

The diversity of the geographical origins of people in this category is reflected in the ethnicities recorded in the optional text box on the census form. The main ethnicities recorded were Filipino (23 per cent), Japanese (21 per cent), Vietnamese (11 per cent), Arab (11 per cent), Middle Eastern (6 per cent) and North African (4 per cent).

Age and sex profile

Four in five (78 per cent) of this category were of working age, with 19 per cent aged under 16 and only 3 per cent over 65. Members of the Other ethnic group born in the UK and Europe were most likely to be under 16 (61 per cent and 58 per cent respectively). African-born respondents had the oldest age profile with only 8 per cent aged under 16.

Although there were marginally more men than women in the Other ethnic group (55 per cent compared to 45 per cent), the distribution varied according to the birth country, with 65 per cent of migrants from the North East Pacific Rim being female, whereas 63 per cent of those born in South Asia were male.

Religions

The religious affiliation of the Other ethnic group is Christian (33 per cent), Muslim (26 per cent) and Buddhist (15 per cent), with 14 per cent stating that they had no religion.

The Mixed ethnic groups

Total population in Britain: 677,000
Proportion of all people in Britain: 1.2 per cent

Source: Census 2001, Office for National Statistics; Census 2001, General Register Office for Scotland

The Mixed category was included for the first time in the 2001 census. The four groups, White and Black Caribbean, White and Black African, White and Asian and Other Mixed, were developed to reflect the presence of children of inter-ethnic partnerships. In Scotland there was only a Mixed ethnic category and a write-in box. Before the 2001 census the assumption had been that people from Mixed ethnic groups preferred to identify themselves with one of their parental ethnicities. The majority of people who identified themselves as in a Mixed ethnic group were born in the UK (79 per cent). In England and Wales the largest of the Mixed ethnic categories was White and Black Caribbean (237,000 people), followed by White and Asian (189,000), Other Mixed groups (156,000) and White and Black African (79,000).

A third (33 per cent) of people with Mixed ethnic identities lived in London, although the likelihood of living there was greater among older people than among younger people with this identity (32 per cent of 16–24s, compared with 38 per cent of over 25s). There was also a sizeable Mixed ethnic community in the South East and the North West.

Age profile

The Mixed ethnic groups have the lowest age profile of any ethnic group, with 50 per cent under the age of 16. The White and Black Caribbean group was the youngest, with 58 per cent under the age of 16.

Religions

Among members of the Mixed ethnic group, Christianity was the most common religion (52 per cent), with 10 per cent identifying themselves as Muslim and 23 per cent identifying themselves as having no religion.

The Indian group

Total population in Britain: 1,051,844
Proportion of all people in Britain: 1.8 per cent

Source: Census 2001, Office for National Statistics; Census 2001, General Register Office for Scotland

Indian is the largest ethnic minority group in Britain. The group may include people whose place of origin, since partition of the Indian subcontinent, has been in Pakistan or since division of Pakistan, in Bangladesh. Slightly less than half of the Indian population (45.9 per cent) was born in the UK, a third (34.6 per cent) in India and about a sixth (16 per cent) in Africa. The Indian population is not homogenous, it contains a variety of regional and religious groups including Indians from Kenya, Uganda and Tanzania who came to Britain as British passport-holders in the 1960s and 1970s to escape 'Africanization' policies.

Patterns of migration

There has been an Indian population in Britain since the eighteenth century. Mini-waves of migration occurred when sailors recruited into the British Navy during the First World War settled in the East End of London and in the 1920s when single males from the Punjab settled in London and other industrial areas. The largest wave of migration was in the 1950s and 1960s. The division of the Indian subcontinent along largely religious lines in 1947 led to violence and disorder in which millions died and 13 million people fled from their homes to seek safety with their own religious majority.

In Britain the combination of post-Second World War reconstruction and a growing British economy had led to labour shortages. Migrants from Punjab, Gujarat, Sylhet and Kashmir in particular travelled to Britain, some attracted by the advertisements placed in Indian newspapers, to work in short-staffed factories. Where these workers settled was largely dictated by the demands of the economy. This is reflected in the distribution of the Indian population in Britain today. It is less concentrated around the capital than are some other minority ethnic groups, with large populations in the West Midlands, East Midlands and South East. Leicester in the East Midlands is home to a particularly large population of people of Indian ethnicity (72,000) who comprise 25.7 of the total population. It is predicted that by the time of the 2011 census it will be the first city in Britain with a majority non-white population.

Languages

The languages spoken by Indians in Britain tend to reflect their regions of origin. Hindi with English is India's official language, but is largely spoken by North Indians. Sikhs from the Punjab speak Punjabi. Although it has a different script, Punjabi shares many common elements with Hindi and has a common ancestor with Sanskrit. The same is true of Gujarati and Bengali. Indians with origins in the state of Gujarat are likely to speak Gujarati and this is often the language of East African Asians in the UK. Indians in Britain may also speak Marathi, Multani, Sindhi or Tamil.

Religions

Roughly half (45 per cent) of Indians in Britain are Hindu. Sikhs make up a third (29 per cent), Muslims a sixth (13 per cent), one in twenty Christian (5 per cent), and there are also Indian Buddhists and Jains. For the purposes of the Race Relations Act 1976, the courts have ruled that Sikhs, unlike other religious groups found in India, also constitute an ethnic group.

Age and sex profile

Post-war migration from India was at first overwhelmingly male; family reunion and mortality has cancelled out any imbalance and the population is now split evenly between men and women. The age profile of the Indian group is younger than that of the White British, but older than that of the other ethnicities in the Asian group, with the majority in the age bracket 20–50.

The Pakistani group

Total population in Britain: 747,000
Proportion of all people in Britain: 1.3 per cent

Source: Census 2001, Office for National Statistics; Census 2001, General Register Office for Scotland

Pakistan was created in 1947 by the partition of the Indian subcontinent and, until 1971, included East Pakistan – the territory that is now Bangladesh. Mass migration from Pakistan began in earnest in the 1960s and was characterized by single male migrants of working age. Two factors contributed significantly to the migration. First, the partition of India along religious lines led to widespread violence and internal migration as people fled to either Pakistan or India depending on their religious affiliation. It is thought that many displaced Pakistanis travelled to Britain in the years after this. Second, in the 1960s the creation of the Mangla Dam in North West Pakistan led to the displacement of a further 100,000 people in Pakistan and many villagers used the compensation money to travel to Britain to find work.

In 2001, 40 per cent of the Pakistani population was born in Pakistan and 55 per cent were born in the UK, indicating much of the growth in the ethnic group has been the result of births rather than immigration. The largest concentration of Pakistanis is in London, with large populations in the West Midlands, Yorkshire and the Humber and the North West. This reflects the distribution of the first group of migrants who settled in major industrial centres where they were most likely to find employment.

Languages

Urdu, essentially the same language as the Hindi spoken in India, but written in Arabic script and influenced more by Persian-Arabic vocabulary, is the main language of the Pakistani population in Britain. Some speak Punjabi. The latter language is also spoken by the Punjabi Sikhs, because the Punjab region was divided during partition.

Religions

The largely Muslim character of Pakistan is reflected in the religious make-up of the Pakistani community in Britain with 92 per cent stating their adherence to this religion.

Age profile

According to the 2001 census the Pakistani population has a youthful age profile, with 35 per cent under the age of 16 and only 4 per cent aged over 65. The sex distribution for Pakistanis up to the age of 65 is typical of the population as a whole, with an even distribution between genders, but after 65 there are more men than women (55 per cent compared with 45 per cent). This may be a reflection of spousal age differences, with men tending to be older than their wives.

The Bangladeshi group

Total population in Britain: 282,811
Proportion of all people in Britain: 0.5 per cent

Source: Census 2001, Office for National Statistics; Census 2001, General Register Office for Scotland

Bangladesh was formed in 1971 from an area that since 1947 had been East Pakistan. Before partition, what is now Bangladesh had been part of the Indian region of Bengal. Although some migration occurred before 1960, the first major wave of arrivals from Bangladesh began in the mid-1960s and was mainly of working-age men. The majority came from the rural area of Sylhet in the north-east of the country, and today many Bangladeshis in Britain still speak a distinct Sylheti dialect. These first male migrants tended to wait longer than their Pakistani and Indian counterparts before bringing their families to the UK and it was not until the 1980s that there was rapid expansion in the population as wives and dependants began to join their husbands in Britain. A large number of the early Bangladeshi migrants settled in East London, where they worked mainly in the garment industry, and today about three-quarters of Britain's Bangladeshis still live in the East London Borough of Tower Hamlets. In 2001, just over half (52 per cent) of people in this group were born in Bangladesh and 45 per cent in Britain.

Religions

Nine out of ten (92 per cent) Bangladeshis classify themselves as Muslim, a similar proportion to that among Pakistani British.

Age and sex profile

The Bangladeshi population is one of the youngest in Britain, with 38 per cent aged under 16 and only 3 per cent aged over 65. The median age for Bangladeshis in Britain is 21, the lowest for any ethnicity with the exception of Mixed, which reflects a range of factors including the high proportion of women of childbearing age, their recent immigration to Britain and a preference for larger families.

There is also a marked disparity between the numbers of men and women at older ages, with men outnumbering women two to one at age 65 and above. This imbalance could be due to the tendency for men to marry women younger than themselves and to emigrate before their families.

Languages

The main language spoken by Bangladeshis, Bengali, is also spoken by people from the Indian state of West Bengal. It is one of the widest-spoken languages in the world based on the number of speakers.

The Other Asian group

Total population in Britain: 247,470
Proportion of all people in Britain: 0.4 per cent

Source: Census 2001, Office for National Statistics; Census 2001, General Register Office for Scotland

Of people classifying themselves as Other Asian, 31 per cent were born in the UK, 24 per cent were born in Sri Lanka and 16 per cent were born in a Middle Eastern country, mostly in Iran (7 per cent) and Iraq (4 per cent). People born in Europe, North America, South American and Oceania also described themselves as Other Asian.

The choice of ethnicity among Other Asians was generally the same as country of birth, with 34 per cent specifying Sri Lankan, 17 per cent specifying a Middle Eastern country and 13 per cent stating they were British Asian. The number of people identifying themselves as Asian British or Asian English was 32 per cent among Other Asians born in the UK and it is likely that most are second- and third-generation descendants of Pakistani, Bangladeshi and Indian migrants.

People who describe themselves as Other Asian live in all British regions, with over half, 133,058, in London and sizeable concentrations in the North West, Yorkshire and the Humber, South East, and in the East and West Midlands.

Age and sex profile

The Other Asian population is largely of working age (71 per cent), with about a quarter (24 per cent) under 16 years of age, and 5 per cent aged over 65. The age profile varies according to the place of birth, with only 42 per cent of UK-born Other Asians of working age, while those born in other nations tended to have between 60 and 92 per cent of people in that age group.

The Other Asian group has slightly more men than women (55 per cent), with the gender difference considerably greater among those born in Iraq and Nepal (where men made up 62 and 69 per cent of the Other Asian population respectively).

Religions

The religious affiliation of the Other Asian group is varied, with 37 per cent Muslims, 27 per cent Hindus and 13 per cent Christians. There were also small numbers of Sikhs, Jews and people with no religion.

The White British group

Total population in Britain: 50,366,497
Proportion of all people in Britain: 88 per cent

Source: Census 2001, Office for National Statistics; Census 2001, General Register Office for Scotland

The 'indigenous' population of Britain – English, Scottish and Welsh – is classified in the census in England and Wales as White British. The majority of people identified as this group, 98 per cent, were born in the UK. In Scotland, White British is not a census category; instead there is a choice of White Scottish and Other White British. The figures in this text are a conflation of the categories from the Census 2001 Scotland and the White British category from the Census 2001 England and Wales.

Age profile

The White British population has an older profile than most other groups, with a high proportion of people above retirement age. There are fairly equal numbers of men and women, although as the population gets older women outnumber men, which reflects their longer average life expectancy. There are a couple of distinct surges in the population among people in their 50s and 30s, which is the result of the baby boom after the Second World War and again in the 1960s.

Religions

Historically Britain has been a Christian country, and 76 per cent of the White British population continue to describe themselves as Christians. A significant number, 15 per cent, state they have no religion. The third largest group among White Britons is Jewish and, although they make up only 0.4 per cent of the ethnic groups, they comprise the majority, 84 per cent, of Jews in Britain.

The White Irish group

Total population in Britain: 691,000
Proportion of all people in Britain: 1.2 per cent

Source: Census 2001, Office for National Statistics; Census 2001, General Register Office for Scotland

Britain has historically been one of the favoured destinations for Irish migrants. For hundreds of years Britain offered the prospect of financial betterment to people living in poverty in Ireland. This was especially true in the nineteenth century when the Industrial Revolution led to a period of economic growth and migrants from Ireland were virtually guaranteed work in construction or the factories. The deprivations of the Great Famine (1845–50) also encouraged people to cross the Irish Sea. Throughout the nineteenth and twentieth century, migration continued and the introduction of immigration quotas in the USA in the 1930s resulted in a further increase in the numbers coming to Britain. There has also been a long tradition of migration by Irish writers and artists, which has seen Jonathan Swift, Oscar Wilde, George Bernard Shaw and Francis Bacon, among others, absorbed into British cultural consciousness.

Patterns of migration

Historically Liverpool was the first point of arrival for Irish migrants, and in 1861 a quarter of the city's population was Irish-born. The major industrial centres, particularly London but also Manchester, London and Glasgow, housed significant Irish populations and this is still true today.

Despite this mass migration from Ireland, the number of people identifying themselves as Irish in the 2001 census was relatively small. This is thought to be the result of a number of factors: people returning to Ireland; the unwillingness of people born in Ireland or their descendants to identify themselves as Irish (this is especially likely for people born in Northern Ireland); and because many children in houses headed by White Irish people were identified as White British.

The fact that many people of Irish origin, but not birth, now identify themselves as White British rather than White Irish distinguishes the Irish in Britain from many non-white ethnic groups in which British-born descendants tend to keep their parents' ethnic classification. It also skews the age profile of the White Irish population, as only 1 in every 16 members of the community are under the age of 16.

Religions

The White Irish population has the largest proportion of Christians of any ethnic group in Britain: 86 per cent identified themselves as such.

The Other White group

Total population in Britain: 1,423,471
Proportion of all people in Britain: 2.5 per cent

Source: Census 2001, Office for National Statistics; Census 2001, General Register Office for Scotland

The category Other White does not comprise a single ethnic group but is instead a method of identification for white people who are not represented by other white census categories.

This means that Other White contains a diverse collection of people with different countries of birth, religions and languages.

Four out of five members of the Other White group were born overseas, with a third (34 per cent) born in Western Europe. At 215,113, the German-born population in Britain is the third largest foreign-born population in Britain after Indians and Pakistanis. One in seven (14 per cent) of the Other White group were born in Eastern Europe, and one in ten (10 per cent) were born in North America.

Age profile

The Other White group is largely of working age, with only one in ten aged over 65 and one in seven under 16. This does vary according to the stated country of birth, with people born in the

UK being disproportionately young. Polish and Italian respondents had a larger proportion of over 65s, which reflects the migration of Poles and Italians to Britain after the Second World War.

Patterns of migration

In the period 1991–2001, the number of Poles in Britain declined, but since Polish accession to the EU in 2004 this trend has reversed and figures from the Home Office reveal that 264,560 Poles registered to work in Britain between 2004 and 2006. The majority of these new Polish migrants to Britain are of working age (82 per cent aged between 16 and 34), and the majority are employed.

Religions

A wide number of religions are represented in the Other White group. The largest faith group, 63 per cent, identified themselves as Christian, with 16 per cent defining themselves as without religion, 9 per cent as Muslims, and 2 per cent as Jewish.

5

Ethnic diversity in UK regions

London

The London region is, by some distance, the most ethnically diverse in Britain. People from minority ethnic groups made up 40 per cent of its population at the time of the 2001 census.

Greater London is the metropolitan area which includes the City of London and the 32 London boroughs. The average population of each borough is around 220,000. The region has a population of over 7.1 million and covers an area of 1,579 square kilometres. The population density is 4,761 people per square kilometre, more than ten times that of any other English region. In 2001, 25 per cent of people living in Greater London were born abroad, up from 19 per cent in 1991.

All but one of the top 25 local authorities in the Office for National Statistics' 'league table' of ethnic diversity were London boroughs. Only 9 of the 32 boroughs were considered less than 'highly diverse' – that is, a less than 50 per cent chance that 2 people chosen at random will belong to the same ethnic group.

On average, for every 1,000 people in London:

597 are White British
120 are Asian
114 are White non-British
109 are Black
32 are of mixed race
11 are Chinese

Source: Office for National Statistics, BBC

Population by ethnic group: London

Population: 7,172,091

Ethnic group/sub-group		*Population*	*Proportion compared to national average*
White		5,103,203	71.1% 90.9% (national average)
	British	4,287,861	59.7% 86.9% (national average)
	Irish	220,488	3.07% 1.27% (national average)
	Other	594,854	8.29% 2.66% (national average)
Mixed		226,111	3.15% 1.30% (national average)
	White and Black Caribbean	70,928	0.98% 0.47% (national average)
	White and Black African	34,182	0.47% 0.15% (national average)
	White and Asian	59,984	0.83% 0.37% (national average)
	Other Mixed	61,057	0.85% 0.30% (national average)
Asian		866,693	12.0% 4.57% (national average)
	Indian	436,993	6.09% 2.09% (national average)
	Pakistani	142,749	1.99% 1.43% (national average)
	Bangladeshi	153,893	2.14% 0.56% (national average)
	Other Asian	133,058	1.85% 0.48% (national average)
Black		782,849	10.9% 2.30% (national average)
	Caribbean	343,567	4.79% 1.14% (national average)
	African	378,933	5.28% 0.96% (national average)

Ethnic group/sub-group	*Population*	*Proportion compared to national average*
Other Black	60,349	0.84% 0.19% (national average)
Chinese	80,201	1.11% 0.44% (national average)
Other ethnic group	113,034	1.57% 0.43% (national average)

Source: Census 2001, Office for National Statistics

Within Greater London, more than 50 ethnic groups are represented in numbers of 10,000 or more. Nearly three-quarters of England's total Black African population live in London, as do six out of ten Black Caribbeans, half the Bangladeshi population, one in four Indians, a third each of England's White Irish, Mixed and Chinese populations, and one in five Pakistanis.

A constantly evolving city

There is a marked difference in concentrations of people from ethnic minorities between inner London and outer London. In inner London a little over half of all residents are white and of British ethnic origin, but for the latter the proportion rises to two-thirds.

London's ethnic make-up is constantly evolving. For centuries, the city has been the first destination for most people migrating to Britain. Today, the fastest growing ethnic minority groups in London are no longer Asian and Caribbean people; over the last decade, White Europeans and African people have formed the majority of new arrivals. According to the 2001 census, the number of black people of African origin living in London has, for the first time, overtaken that of people of Caribbean descent.

South East England

The South East is the third most ethnically diverse of the nine regions that make up England. Nine per cent of people living here

On average, for every 1,000 people in South East England:

913 are White British
38 are White non-British
23 are Asian
11 are of mixed race
7 are Black
4 are Chinese

Source: Office for National Statistics, BBC

are from ethnic minority groups, but this figure still lags a long way behind that of London (40 per cent) and the West Midlands (14 per cent). Of people living in the South East, 7.3 per cent were born abroad. This is very close to the national average of 7.5 per cent. The figure for 1991 was 5.7 per cent.

More people live in the South East – a fraction over 8 million – than any English region. In geographic terms, it is the third largest, covering an area of 19,096 square kilometres, and has a population density of 419 people per square kilometre. Within the region, there are considerable contrasts in terms of its ethnic make-up.

The towns and cities that are geographically closest to London – such as Reading and Slough – tend to have much greater proportions of ethnic minority residents, while those further away, on the south coast, have much smaller ones. For example, Slough has an even smaller proportion of residents from the White British group than London (58 per cent against 60 per cent), while in Dover and Portsmouth, the figure increases to 96 per cent and 92 per cent respectively.

The main reason for this is the recent trend for many people from ethnic minority groups to move further out of the London area as they have become more affluent, following the pattern of many people of White British ethnicity. Areas towards the south coast, on the other hand, have been less affected by this trend, although there are exceptions – the port city of Southampton has historically had large migrant communities, particularly from South Asia.

This 'halo effect' from London manifests itself in other ways within the region's ethnic profile. Areas in the 'stockbroker belt', such as Guildford and Godalming, have disproportionately large numbers of residents from the White Other groups, suggesting large concentrations of wealthy migrants from Europe and North America. Reading, which is often considered England's 'technology capital', due to the large number of multinational telecommunications, electronics and IT firms based there, has higher proportions of almost all ethnic groups compared to the national average, which highlights the great diversity of the people who are drawn to work in those industries.

Education has played a part in the growth of non-White British populations. Some of the greatest recent increases have been in places like Oxford, where the university regards fee-paying foreign students as the key to its future. Oxford, in fact, has some of the highest proportions of residents from the White Other, Chinese and Other ethnic groups of anywhere in England.

The largest ethnic minority group in the South East is White Other. Together with the South West, this region is one of only two in England where this group is more numerous than the Asian or Black groups. More than 221,000 people indicated this as their ethnic origin in the 2001 census. As mentioned above, this is likely to be due to a number of reasons, including employment and education.

Asian people form the second most populous ethnic minority group: over 185,000 people, or 2.3 per cent of the population. Slough alone is home to more than 33,000 people from this group. There are roughly a third more Indians than Pakistanis throughout the region as a whole, and only in a few places – such as Reading – does the population of the latter exceed that of the former.

Black people live in far fewer numbers in the South East compared to the two groups above; there are three times more Asians, and nearly four times more White Other residents than the 57,000 black people living here. Reading and Slough each

Population by ethnic group: South East

Population: 8,000,645

Ethnic group/sub-group		*Population*	*Proportion compared to national average*
White		7,608,989	95.1% 90.9% (national average)
	British	7,304,678	91.3% 86.9% (national average)
	Irish	82,405	1.02% 1.27% (national average)
	Other	221,906	2.77% 2.66% (national average)
Mixed		85,779	1.07% 1.30% (national average)
	White and Black Caribbean	23,742	0.29% 0.47% (national average)
	White and Black African	9,493	0.11% 0.15% (national average)
	White and Asian	29,977	0.37% 0.37% (national average)
	Other Mixed	22,567	0.28% 0.30% (national average)
Asian		186,615	2.33% 4.57% (national average)
	Indian	89,219	1.11% 2.09% (national average)
	Pakistani	58,520	0.73% 1.43% (national average)
	Bangladeshi	15,358	0.19% 0.56% (national average)
	Other Asian	23,518	0.29% 0.48% (national average)
Black		56,914	0.71% 2.30% (national average)
	Caribbean	27,452	0.34% 1.14% (national average)
	African	24,582	0.30% 0.96% (national average)

Ethnic group/sub-group	*Population*	*Proportion compared to national average*
Other Black	4,880	0.06% 0.19% (national average)
Chinese	33,089	0.41% 0.44% (national average)
Other ethnic group	29,259	0.36% 0.43% (national average)

Source: Census 2001, Office for National Statistics

account for about 10 per cent of this number, but the typical proportion elsewhere is between 0.5 and 1 per cent – four times less than the national average.

South West England

The South West is one of the least ethnically diverse of the nine English regions. Only the North East has a greater proportion of White British residents than the 95.3 per cent in the South West.

According to the 2001 census, 4.4 per cent of the South West's population were born abroad. Although low by national standards, this nonetheless represented an increase of 34 per cent compared to the census in 1991, when only 3.5 per cent were foreign-born.

On average, for every 1,000 people in South West England:

953 are White British
24 are White non-British
8 are Asian
7 are of mixed race
4 are Black
3 are Chinese

Source: Office for National Statistics, BBC

Population by ethnic group: South West

Population: 4,928,434

Ethnic group/sub-group		*Population*	*Proportion compared to national average*
White		4,815,316	97.7% 90.9% (national average)
	British	4,701,602	95.3% 86.9% (national average)
	Irish	32,484	0.65% 1.27% (national average)
	Other	81,230	1.64% 2.66% (national average)
Mixed		37,371	0.75% 1.30% (national average)
	White and Black Caribbean	13,343	0.27% 0.47% (national average)
	White and Black African	3,917	0.07% 0.15% (national average)
	White and Asian	11,198	0.22% 0.37% (national average)
	Other Mixed	8,913	0.18% 0.30% (national average)
Asian		32,800	0.66% 4.57% (national average)
	Indian	16,394	0.33% 2.09% (national average)
	Pakistani	6,729	0.13% 1.43% (national average)
	Bangladeshi	4,816	0.09% 0.56% (national average)
	Other Asian	4,861	0.09% 0.48% (national average)
Black		20,920	0.42% 2.30% (national average)
	Caribbean	12,405	0.25% 1.14% (national average)
	African	6,171	0.12% 0.96% (national average)

Ethnic group/sub-group	*Population*	*Proportion compared to national average*
Other Black	2,344	0.04% 0.19% (national average)
Chinese	12,722	0.25% 0.44% (national average)
Other ethnic group	9,305	0.18% 0.43% (national average)

Source: Census 2001, Office for National Statistics

The South West region had a total population of 4.9 million, according to the 2001 census. It covers an area of 23,829 square kilometres, making it the largest of England's nine regions. It is also the most sparsely populated, with an average of just 207 people living on each square kilometre of land.

Because the South West is a largely rural area, its ethnic minority population does not generally consist of geographically clustered communities, as is typical in many urban areas and some other rural regions. Instead, it is characterized by a wide diversity of rural dwellers living as individuals and families, not usually as communities. This has meant that many people of minority ethnic origin living in the South West, especially rural Devon and Cornwall, are not present in numbers large enough to support the local provision of culturally specific goods and services, such as halal or kosher food, for example.

People from the White Other group form the largest minority ethnic group in the region. More than 81,000 people, or 1.6 per cent of the population, indicated this as their ethnic origin in the 2001 census. Just three other regions in England – London, the South East and the East of England – have higher proportions of this group.

The next most populous group is made up of people in the Mixed category. The South West is the only English region where this group is proportionally greater than black and Asian people, although in numerical terms the Mixed population here is smaller than that of any other region apart from the North East. One reason for this is the large Mixed populations in Bristol and Gloucester – more than 2 per cent of both cities' residents – which skews the overall proportion somewhat.

No other region in England has a smaller proportion of Asian people (just 0.7 per cent) within its total population than the South West. This is little more than half the proportion of the next lowest (the North East, at 1.3 per cent).

Only the North East has proportionally fewer black residents. In the South West, the Black group makes up just 0.4 per cent of the population. The difference compared to the national average is less marked for black people than Asians, however, because every region in England – apart from London and the West Midlands – has a black population that makes up less than 1 per cent of all residents.

East of England

According to the 2001 census, the East of England is home to 5.4 million people, ranking it fourth on the list of England's most populous regions.

Overall, in terms of its ethnic diversity, the East of England region falls slightly below the average for the country as a whole.

In 2001, 6.1 per cent of people living in the East Midlands were born abroad, up from 5.1 per cent in 1991.

On average, for every 1,000 people in the East of England:

914 are White British
37 are White non-British
23 are Asian
11 are of mixed race
9 are Black
4 are Chinese

Source: Office for National Statistics, BBC

Population by ethnic group: East of England

Population: 5,388,140

Ethnic group/sub-group		*Population*	*Proportion compared to national average*
White		5,125,003	95.1% 90.9% (national average)
	British	4,927,343	91.4% 86.9% (national average)
	Irish	61,208	1.13% 1.27% (national average)
	Other	136,452	2.53% 2.66% (national average)
Mixed		57,984	1.07% 1.30% (national average)
	White and Black Caribbean	19,882	0.36% 0.47% (national average)
	White and Black African	6,109	0.11% 0.15% (national average)
	White and Asian	17,385	0.32% 0.37% (national average)
	Other Mixed	14,608	0.27% 0.30% (national average)
Asian		121,752	2.25% 4.57% (national average)
	Indian	51,035	0.94% 2.09% (national average)
	Pakistani	38,790	0.71% 1.43% (national average)
	Bangladeshi	18,503	0.34% 0.56% (national average)
	Other Asian	13,424	0.24% 0.48% (national average)
Black		48,464	0.89% 2.30% (national average)
	Caribbean	26,199	0.48% 1.14% (national average)
	African	16,968	0.31% 0.96% (national average)

Ethnic group/sub-group	*Population*	*Proportion compared to national average*
Other Black	5,297	0.09% 0.19% (national average)
Chinese	20,385	0.37% 0.44% (national average)
Other ethnic group	14,552	0.27% 0.43% (national average)

Source: Census 2001, Office for National Statistics

Only one ethnic group – White British, at 91 per cent – is represented here at a proportion greater than the national average, and its share of Asian residents is among the lowest of the nine English regions.

The region includes one large town – Luton, which is remarkable for its ethnic diversity. With less than two-thirds (64 per cent) of its population coming from the White British group, it ranks behind only London, Leicester and Slough on the Office for National Statistics' ethnic diversity index. It is home to more than a quarter of all Asian people living in the region, despite accounting for just 3 per cent of the region's total population.

Asians are not, however, the largest ethnic minority group in the region. That distinction goes to the White Other group, which, at 136,000 people, accounts for 2.5 per cent of the population of the East of England.

There are three significant reasons for this. The first is the large number of US and German-born military personnel serving in the area. Nearly 65,000 US and German citizens lived in the area at the time of the 2001 census, the vast majority of whom would have described themselves as being of White Other ethnic origin.

Second, the region attracts a large number of overseas students, as it contains some of Britain's largest universities, including Cambridge, where people from the White Other group make up nearly 10 per cent of all residents. Third, this region has been one of the leading destinations for non-EU European migrants, due to the ready availability of work within its large agricultural sector; even in 2001, before EU expansion brought still greater numbers of migrant workers to the area, some parts, such as West Thurrock, saw their proportions of foreign-born residents double compared to ten years previously.

Although the proportion of black people living in the region is less than 1 per cent this is still one of the highest concentrations of this ethnic group outside London and the West Midlands. Of the 48,000 black people living here, about 60 per cent are of Caribbean origin, nearly a quarter of whom live in Luton, with about 10 per cent in Milton Keynes. Milton Keynes is remarkable for the fact that it mirrors almost perfectly the ethnic make-up of England as a whole across all 16 Census 2001 categories.

East Midlands

Nine per cent of people living in the East Midlands region at the time of the 2001 census were of minority ethnic origin. Of the eight other English regions, only London and the West Midlands had a higher proportion of non-White British residents. In 2001, 5.4 per cent of people living in the East Midlands were born abroad, up from 4.5 per cent in 1991.

A total of 4.1 million people live in the East Midlands, and only the North East has a smaller population among England's nine regions. In terms of physical size, it is the fourth largest, covering

On average, for every 1,000 people in East Midlands:

912 are White British
40 are Asian
22 are White non-British
10 are of mixed race
9 are Black
3 are Chinese

Source: Office for National Statistics, BBC

an area of 15,627 square kilometres. On average, 267 people live per square kilometre.

As in many other English regions, ethnic minority populations are not evenly distributed across the East Midlands. There are cities which are extremely diverse, such as Leicester – which is widely tipped to become the first city in Europe with a majority non-white population at some point during the next decade – Derby and Nottingham. But in many places elsewhere, such as Mansfield, Chesterfield and Lincoln, the non-White British population is much smaller, typically between 3 per cent and 4 per cent.

The three main cities in the region are ethnically diverse in quite different ways. The most striking aspect of Leicester, for example, is its very large population of Indians (72,000 people, or more than a quarter of all residents); Derby is notable for its large proportion of Indian Sikhs (the vast majority of Indians living in England are Hindus); while Nottingham has one of the largest proportions of black residents (particularly those of Caribbean origin) outside London.

Asian people form by far the largest ethnic minority group in the East Midlands. Their numbers are roughly equal to the combined total of all other minority ethnic groups in the region.

This is largely due to the 'Leicester effect' – this city alone accounts for half of all Asians living in the region, including 60 per cent of all people of Indian origin. Not all Asian sub-groups are as well represented though; there are proportionally fewer Bangladeshis (less than 0.2 per cent of the population) living here than in all but one of the other eight English regions.

People from the White Other category make up the second largest ethnic minority group in the East Midlands, numbering 57,000, or 1.4 per cent of the population. This is about average for the nine English regions.

Although black people make up less than 1 per cent of the region's population, this is nonetheless one of the highest proportions outside London; only the neighbouring West Midlands region has a greater percentage of black residents within its population outside the capital. Of the nearly 40,000 black people living here, more than 60 per cent are of Caribbean origin.

Population by ethnic group: East Midlands

Population: 4,172,174

Ethnic group/sub-group		*Population*	*Proportion compared to national average*
White		3,900,380	93.4% 90.9% (national average)
	British	3,807,731	91.2% 86.9% (national average)
	Irish	35,478	0.85% 1.27% (national average)
	Other	57,171	1.37% 2.66% (national average)
Mixed		43,141	1.03% 1.30% (national average)
	White and Black Caribbean	20,658	0.49% 0.47% (national average)
	White and Black African	3,426	0.08% 0.15% (national average)
	White and Asian	11,176	0.26% 0.37% (national average)
	Other Mixed	7,881	0.18% 0.30% (national average)
Asian		168,913	4.04% 4.57% (national average)
	Indian	122,346	2.93% 2.09% (national average)
	Pakistani	27,829	0.66% 1.43% (national average)
	Bangladeshi	6,923	0.16% 0.56% (national average)
	Other Asian	11,815	0.28% 0.48% (national average)
Black		39,477	0.94% 2.30% (national average)
	Caribbean	26,684	0.63% 1.14% (national average)
	African	9,165	0.21% 0.96% (national average)

Ethnic group/sub-group	*Population*	*Proportion compared to national average*
Other Black	3,628	0.08% 0.19% (national average)
Chinese	12,910	0.30% 0.44% (national average)
Other ethnic group	7,353	0.17% 0.43% (national average)

Source: Census 2001, Office for National Statistics

West Midlands

The West Midlands is by far the most ethnically diverse English region outside London, according to the 2001 census data. Nearly one in seven of its population (13.9 per cent) are from ethnic groups other than White British. In 2001, 6.5 per cent of people living in the West Midlands were born abroad, up from 5.3 per cent in 1991.

Nearly 5.3 million people lived in the region at the time of the last census. It covers a geographical area of 13,004 square kilometres, and has a population density of 405 people per square kilometre.

The West Midlands is the only English region, apart from London, where the proportion of residents from the White British group falls below the national average of 87 per cent.

On average, for every 1,000 people in West Midlands:

861 are White British
73 are Asian
26 are White non-British
20 are Black
14 are of mixed race
3 are Chinese

Source: Office for National Statistics, BBC

Population by ethnic group: West Midlands

Population: 5,267,308

Ethnic group/sub-group		*Population*	*Proportion compared to national average*
White		4,674,296	88.7% 90.9% (national average)
	British	4,537,892	86.1% 86.9% (national average)
	Irish	73,136	1.38% 1.27% (national average)
	Other	63,268	1.20% 2.66% (national average)
Mixed		73,225	1.39% 1.30% (national average)
	White and Black Caribbean	39,782	0.75% 0.47% (national average)
	White and Black African	3,683	0.06% 0.15% (national average)
	White and Asian	18,160	0.34% 0.37% (national average)
	Other Mixed	11,600	0.22% 0.30% (national average)
Asian		385,573	7.32% 4.57% (national average)
	Indian	178,691	3.39% 2.09% (national average)
	Pakistani	154,550	2.93% 1.43% (national average)
	Bangladeshi	31,401	0.59% 0.56% (national average)
	Other Asian	20,931	0.39% 0.48% (national average)
Black		104,032	1.97% 2.30% (national average)
	Caribbean	82,282	1.56% 1.14% (national average)
	African	11,985	0.22% 0.96% (national average)

Ethnic group/sub-group	*Population*	*Proportion compared to national average*
Other Black	9,765	0.18% 0.19% (national average)
Chinese	16,099	0.30% 0.44% (national average)
Other ethnic group	14,083	0.26% 0.43% (national average)

Source: Census 2001, Office for National Statistics

Birmingham, England's second largest city and the main population centre in the West Midlands, is second only to the capital in terms of its ethnic diversity. With nearly 200,000 Asian and 60,000 black residents, Birmingham is home to more people from these groups than most entire regions of England (excluding London, only the Yorkshire and The Humber region has more Asian residents, and none has more black residents).

There are nearly 400,000 people of South Asian origin living in the West Midlands (7.3 per cent of all residents). The region is home to one in six of all Asians in Britain. Aside from Birmingham, where 20 per cent of the population is Asian, there are also very large Asian communities in Wolverhampton, where people from this group form 14 per cent of the local population, and in Coventry (11 per cent). There are more Pakistanis living in the West Midlands – 155,000 – than in any other English region, London included. Across the entire region, the population is split fairly evenly between Indians and Pakistanis; at town and city level, though, the tendency is for one group to predominate over the other. In Birmingham, for example, the ratio of Pakistanis to Indians is two to one, while in Wolverhampton there are ten times as many Indians as Pakistanis.

In terms of its black population, the West Midlands is also second only to London, both numerically (104,000 people) and as a proportion of all residents (2 per cent). The latter figure is nearly twice that of the next region in the list, the South East.

Fifteen per cent of all Black Caribbeans living in Britain live in the West Midlands, but only a couple of towns and cities, such as Birmingham and Wolverhampton, have black populations (4.6 per cent and 6.1 per cent of all residents, respectively) significantly above the national average for England.

Nowhere else in the country has a black population been so dominated by the Black Caribbean group; here, they outnumber people of African descent by more than seven to one (contrast this with London, where the Black African population has recently increased to a point where it now exceeds the number of Black Caribbean residents).

Most other minority ethnic groups are represented in the West Midlands in similar proportions to other regions of England. There is, however, a much higher percentage of people from the Mixed White and Black Caribbean group than the national average – nearly 40,000 people, or 0.8 per cent of all residents. In Wolverhampton and Birmingham, this figure is even higher, at between 1.5 per cent and 2 per cent; across the whole of England, only a few inner London boroughs have marginally higher proportions of this group.

Yorkshire and the Humber

Yorkshire and the Humber ranks fifth of the nine English regions in terms of its proportion of minority ethnic residents. About one

On average, for every 1,000 people in Yorkshire and the Humber:

916 are White British
45 are Asian
18 are White non-British
9 are of mixed race
7 are Black
2 are Chinese

Source: Office for National Statistics, BBC

in twelve people living in the region are from ethnic groups other than White British. In 2001, 4.7 per cent of people living in the Yorkshire and Humber region were born abroad, up from 3.7 per cent in 1991.

According to the 2001 census, the Yorkshire and Humber region has a total population of 5.1 million. It is the fifth largest of England's nine regions, covering an area of 15,420 square kilometres, and has a population density of 328 people per square kilometre.

Although there are many large cities and towns in the region, large areas of Yorkshire and the Humber are very rural. This means that the degree of ethnic diversity varies considerably throughout the region, with the vast majority of people from minority ethnic groups concentrated in urban areas. For example, while the three major cities of Leeds, Sheffield and Bradford account for just a third of the region's total population, they are home to 65 per cent of all Asians and 70 per cent of all black people.

There are almost as many Asian people – 222,000 – living in this region than all other minority ethnic groups combined. This figure represents 4.5 per cent of the total population. Only London (12 per cent) and the West Midlands (7.3 per cent) have a greater proportion of Asian residents, although both have far larger Asian populations in numerical terms.

Yorkshire and the Humber is one of only three English regions with more Pakistani residents than Indian ones, and the ratio here – nearly three to one – is far greater than in the North West and the North East. The main reason for this is the remarkably large Pakistani population in Bradford; nearly 68,000 – almost half of all people from this group living in the entire region – live here, where they make up one in seven of all residents. This is the highest proportion of Pakistanis in the total population of any city in Europe. Across the entire region, there are nearly 150,000 people of Pakistani descent; only the West Midlands has a marginally greater number.

The proportions of non-Asian minority ethnic groups in the region are quite small. The White Other group is the second most

Population by ethnic group: Yorkshire and the Humber

Population: 4,964,833

Ethnic group/sub-group		*Population*	*Proportion compared to national average*
White		4,641,263	93.4% 90.9% (national average)
	British	4,551,394	91.6% 86.9% (national average)
	Irish	32,735	0.65% 1.27% (national average)
	Other	57,134	1.15% 2.66% (national average)
Mixed		44,995	0.90% 1.30% (national average)
	White and Black Caribbean	18,187	0.36% 0.47% (national average)
	White and Black African	4,094	0.08% 0.15% (national average)
	White and Asian	14,218	0.28% 0.37% (national average)
	Other Mixed	8,496	0.17% 0.30% (national average)
Asian		222,486	4.48% 4.57% (national average)
	Indian	51,493	1.03% 2.09% (national average)
	Pakistani	146,330	2.94% 1.43% (national average)
	Bangladeshi	12,330	0.24% 0.56% (national average)
	Other Asian	12,333	0.24% 0.48% (national average)
Black		34,262	0.69% 2.30% (national average)
	Caribbean	21,308	0.42% 1.14% (national average)
	African	9,625	0.19% 0.96% (national average)

Ethnic group/sub-group	Population	Proportion compared to national average
Other Black	3,329	0.06% 0.19% (national average)
Chinese	12,340	0.24% 0.44% (national average)
Other ethnic group	9,487	0.19% 0.43% (national average)

Source: Census 2001, Office for National Statistics

populous minority ethnic group, but forms just 1.2 per cent of the population; this is the third lowest proportion among the nine English regions. The proportion of Chinese residents is the joint lowest in England, at just 0.25 per cent of all residents.

Black people make up the third largest minority ethnic group in Yorkshire and the Humber. Proportionally, the Black groups make up 0.7 per cent of the population; this is lower than all but three of the other eight English regions. Out of a total of 34,000 black people in the region, two-thirds are of Caribbean origin. Nearly a third of all black people in the region live in Sheffield, where they form nearly 2 per cent of the local population. Leeds also has a sizeable black population, about 1.5 per cent, but elsewhere numbers are very small – Barnsley, for example, has just 164 black residents out of a total population of 220,000.

North East England

The North East is the least diverse of England's nine regions. At 96.4 per cent, its proportion of White British residents was greater than any other area at the 2001 census, and it had the smallest proportion of minority ethnic residents in 10 of the 16 census categories. In 2001, 2.7 per cent of people living in the North East were born abroad, up from 1.9 per cent in 1991.

On average, for every 1,000 people in North East England:

964 are White British
13 are Asian
12 are White non-British
5 are of mixed race (national average)
2 are Black
2 are Chinese

Source: Office for National Statistics, BBC

In 2001, the North East region had a total population of 2.5 million. This makes it by far the least populous region of England; the East Midlands, which is one place higher in the list, has 4.2 million inhabitants. The North East is the second smallest in terms of area covered, at 8,592 square kilometres. The population density is 293 people per square kilometre of land.

The most diverse town or city in the region is Newcastle, yet even here only its Pakistani, Bangladeshi and Chinese populations are represented in numbers marginally greater than the average for the whole of England.

The region's black population – less than 4,000 people – is especially small, less than 0.2 per cent of the population. This proportion is less than half that of the next lowest region, the South West. In Easington, at the time of the 2001 census, there were only 18 black people within a population of 94,000; it was alone among England's 376 local authorities in recording zero residents in one of the Office for National Statistics' ethnic categories (the Black Other group).

The North East and London are the only two English regions where the Black African population outnumbers the Black Caribbean one (by three to one, in the case of the North East).

The Asian group is by far the largest of all ethnic minorities in the region, at 33,000 people, or 1.3 per cent of all residents. Following the trend elsewhere in northern England, it is Pakistanis who predominate within this group. A third of all Asians in the

Population by ethnic group: North East

Population: 2,515,442

Ethnic group/sub-group		*Population*	*Proportion compared to national average*
White		2,455,416	97.6% 90.9% (national average)
	British	2,425,592	96.4% 86.9% (national average)
	Irish	8,682	0.34% 1.27% (national average)
	Other	21,142	0.84% 2.66% (national average)
Mixed		12,228	0.48% 1.30% (national average)
	White and Black Caribbean	2,783	0.11% 0.47% (national average)
	White and Black African	1,741	0.06% 0.15% (national average)
	White and Asian	4,733	0.18% 0.37% (national average)
	Other Mixed	2,971	0.11% 0.30% (national average)
Asian		33,582	1.33% 4.57% (national average)
	Indian	10,156	0.40% 2.09% (national average)
	Pakistani	14,074	0.55% 1.43% (national average)
	Bangladeshi	6,167	0.24% 0.56% (national average)
	Other Asian	3,185	0.12% 0.48% (national average)
Black		3,953	0.15% 2.30% (national average)
	Caribbean	927	0.03% 1.14% (national average)
	African	2,597	0.10% 0.96% (national average)

Ethnic group/sub-group	*Population*	*Proportion compared to national average*
Other Black	497	0.01% 0.19% (national average)
Chinese	6,048	0.24% 0.44% (national average)
Other ethnic group	4,215	0.16% 0.43% (national average)

Source: Census 2001, Office for National Statistics

region live in Newcastle, where they make up 4.5 per cent of all residents.

Elsewhere, populations tend to be very small; in Durham, for example, which has over 85,000 inhabitants, there are just 62 Pakistanis – one of the lowest proportions anywhere in England.

North West England

Statistically, this region ranks seventh out of the nine English regions in terms of its number of minority ethnic residents. Only the North East and the South West have a greater proportion of people from the White British group (92.1 per cent). Foreign-

On average, for every 1,000 people in North West England:

921 are White British
34 are Asian
23 are White non-British
11 are of mixed race
8 are Black
8 are Chinese

Source: Office for National Statistics, BBC

born people accounted for 4 per cent of the region's population in 2001 – up by 1 per cent from 1991.

On the other hand, some parts of the region – notably Manchester and the Lancashire towns of Blackburn, Preston, Oldham and Burnley – have much larger ethnic minority populations, particularly within the Asian groups.

The North West region has a total population of 6.7 million, according to the 2001 census. Geographically, it is the sixth largest of the nine English regions, covering an area of 14,165 square kilometres. It has a population density of 475 people per square kilometre; only London has a more concentrated population.

Across the region as a whole, there are nearly a quarter of a million Asian people, ranking it behind only London (over 850,000) and the West Midlands (almost 400,000) among all English regions. In Blackburn, one in five residents are of either Indian or Pakistani descent, while Manchester, Oldham and Preston all have Asian populations either close to, or exceeding, 10 per cent of all residents.

These areas in Lancashire are notable for the fact that their large Indian populations are predominantly Gujarati Muslims; most people of Indian descent living in Britain are Hindus.

The entire North West is home to a quarter of England's 133,000 Indian Muslims, but only 1 in 20 and 1 in 50 of the Indian Hindu and Indian Sikh populations respectively.

The English-born Asian population in the North West is mostly descended from people who had arrived in Britain during the 1950s and 1960s, following the partition of the Indian subcontinent after the Second World War. However, the roots of the South Asian population here reach much deeper into history; during the Industrial Revolution of the nineteenth century, workers from the subcontinent were a common sight in the mills and textile factories around the Pennines.

It is interesting to note that the Asian population in the North West is very highly concentrated within the Greater Manchester and Lancashire areas. Even if we move just a little further to the west, to Liverpool – which is only 30 miles from Manchester – or to Stockport, the proportion of Asian residents

Population by ethnic group: North West England

Population: 6,729,764

Ethnic group/sub-group		*Population*	*Proportion compared to national average*
White		6,355,495	94.4% 90.9% (national average)
	British	6,203,043	92.1% 86.9% (national average)
	Irish	77,499	1.15% 1.27% (national average)
	Other	74,953	1.11% 2.66% (national average)
Mixed		62,539	0.92% 1.30% (national average)
	White and Black Caribbean	22,119	0.32% 0.47% (national average)
	White and Black African	9,853	0.14% 0.15% (national average)
	White and Asian	17,223	0.25% 0.37% (national average)
	Other Mixed	13,344	0.19% 0.30% (national average)
Asian		229,875	3.41% 4.57% (national average)
	Indian	72,219	1.07% 2.09% (national average)
	Pakistani	116,968	1.73% 1.43% (national average)
	Bangladeshi	26,003	0.38% 0.56% (national average)
	Other Asian	14,685	0.21% 0.48% (national average)
Black		41,637	0.61% 2.30% (national average)
	Caribbean	20,422	0.30% 1.14% (national average)
	African	15,912	0.23% 0.96% (national average)

Ethnic group/sub-group	*Population*	*Proportion compared to national average*
Other Black	5,303	0.07% 0.19% (national average)
Chinese	26,887	0.39% 0.44% (national average)
Other ethnic group	13,331	0.19% 0.43% (national average)

falls dramatically; barely 1 per cent of Liverpool's population is of Asian origin.

The North West also ranks third among English regions in the size of its Irish population. The 2001 census figures show nearly 80,000 Irish people live in the region.

Paradoxically, the city which is best known for its historically large number of Irish residents, Liverpool, actually lags slightly behind the national average in terms of its proportionate share of this group. This is surprising, as in 1861 a quarter of Liverpool's population was Irish-born, and the city is geographically closer to the Irish mainland than any other English city. In this case, however, the bare statistics from the census are likely to be misleading, as recent research by the Office for National Statistics suggests that many people of Irish origin (but not birth) tended to identify themselves as White British rather than White Irish on census forms.

As in most regions outside London and the West Midlands, black people form a very small minority in the North West: less than 1 per cent of all residents, or just over 40,000 people.

Nearly half of them (18,000) live in Manchester, which is the only town or city in the region to have a proportion of black residents (4.5 per cent) higher than the national average (2.3 per cent). There are more Black Caribbeans than Black Africans living in the region, by a ratio of about three to two.

Wales

Wales is much less ethnically diverse than England; people from minority ethnic groups made up only 4 per cent of its population in 2001, compared to 13 per cent for England. In 2001, 2.7 per cent of people living in Wales were born abroad, up from 2.2 per cent in 1991. Wales is less diverse than Scotland, although like-for-like comparisons are difficult, because Scotland uses a different system of ethnic classification.

On average, for every 1,000 people in Wales:

959 are White British
19 are White non-British
9 are Asian
6 are of mixed race
2 are Black
2 are Chinese

Source: Office for National Statistics, BBC

Wales is the smallest of the three countries that make up Great Britain, both in terms of its physical size and its population. At the time of the 2001 census, there were 2.9 million people living in Wales across an area of 20,779 square kilometres. Its population density of 140 people per square kilometre is lower than any region of England.

The population distribution within Wales is very uneven, as it combines a few large population centres with large areas of sparsely inhabited, mostly rural land. Cardiff, its capital city, is home to more than half of all black people living in Wales, and just under half of its total Asian population. Wales has fewer foreign-born residents than any other nation or region in Britain – just 2.7 per cent of the total population – and also recorded the smallest increase in people born abroad at the 2001 census. Nearly 26,000 Asian people living in Wales in 2001 make this group the largest ethnic minority in the country. The population is split very evenly between Indians and Pakistanis, although in Cardiff

Population by ethnic group: Wales

Population: 2,903,085

Ethnic group/sub-group		*Population*	*Proportion of all residents*
White		2,841,505	97.8%
	British	2,786,605	95.9%
	Irish	17,689	0.60%
	Other	37,211	1.28%
Mixed		17,661	0.60%
	White and Black Caribbean	5,996	0.20%
	White and Black African	2,413	0.08%
	White and Asian	5,001	0.17%
	Other Mixed	4,251	0.14%
Asian		25,448	0.87%
	Indian	8,261	0.28%
	Pakistani	8,287	0.28%
	Bangladeshi	5,436	0.18%
	Other Asian	3,464	0.11%
Black		7,069	0.24%
	Caribbean	2,597	0.08%
	African	3,727	0.12%
	Other Black	745	0.02%
Chinese		6,267	0.21%
Other ethnic group		5,135	0.17%

Source: Census 2001, Office for National Statistics

there is a rapidly growing Bangladeshi population, which now makes up more than a quarter of all Asians in the city. Aside from Cardiff, where 4 per cent of all residents are Asian, the next largest concentration of this group is in Wrexham (2.6 per cent), where Pakistanis predominate.

Although the number of black people living in Wales appears small, amounting to just over 7,000 people or 0.25 per cent of the population, there is some doubt as to whether the Census 2001 data accurately reflect the true size of the black population. For example, the Somali population in Cardiff alone is estimated at anywhere between 4,000 and 10,000 people, and is thought to be the largest concentration of people originating from this country anywhere in Britain. Unlike England, in Wales Black African is the largest black group in the population.

In many parts of Wales, especially in the valleys and to the north of the country, people of colour are a rare sight. In Wrexham, 99 per cent of the population are white, and there are only 164 black people out of a total population of 128,000.

Scotland

In 2001, 3.3 per cent of people living in Scotland were born abroad, up from 2.5 per cent in 1991.

Scotland had a population of just over 5 million people at the time of the 2001 census. It covers an area of 78,772 square kilometres, meaning that, on average, just 64 people live on each square kilometre of Scottish soil (for England the figure is 377, in Wales 140).

Between 1991 and 2001, Scotland's foreign-born population rose by 34 per cent, compared with 29 per cent in England and 24 per cent in Wales.

On average, for every 1,000 people in Scotland:

880 are White Scottish
74 are White (non-Scottish) British
25 are from other white groups, including Irish
11 are Asian
3 are of mixed race
3 are Chinese
2 are Black

Source: Office for National Statistics, BBC

The exact size of the 'other ethnic group' in Scotland in 2006 – five years on from the census – is a matter of some debate. The Commission for Racial Equality in Scotland believes that recent factors, such as migration from recent EU accession countries – notably Poland – means that the true proportion of minority ethnic residents in Scotland is likely to be closer to 4 per cent; twice that of the Census 2001 figure. This mirrors the proportion of school pupils in Scotland who are of minority ethnic origin, according to a school census carried out in September 2005 by the Scottish Executive.

Population by ethnic group: Scotland

Population: 5,062,011

Ethnic group/sub-group		*Population*	*Proportion of all residents*
White		4,960,334	97.9%
	Scottish	4,459,071	88.0%
	Other White British	373,685	7.38%
	White Irish	49,428	0.97%
	Other	78,150	1.54%
Asian		55,007	1.08%
	Indian	15,037	0.29%
	Pakistani	31,793	0.62%
	Bangladeshi	1,981	0.03%
	Other South Asian	6,196	0.12%
Mixed		12,764	0.25%
Black		8,025	0.15%
	Caribbean	1,778	0.03%
	African	5,118	0.10%
	Black Scottish or Other Black	1,129	0.02%
Chinese		16,310	0.32%
Other ethnic group		9,571	0.18%

Source: Office for National Statistics

The ethnic group classifications used in Scotland's census differ slightly from those in England and Wales, most notably in that White Scottish people and Other White British people (mostly people from England and Wales) are counted separately. This latter category forms the largest minority ethnic group in Scotland (7.4 per cent of the population, or roughly 1 in 14 people), although there is considerable variation from area to area; in Edinburgh, 1 in 9 people (11.4 per cent) are from this Other White British category, while in Glasgow the figure is as low as 1 in 30 (3.6 per cent).

Since the 2001 census was carried out, the Scottish Executive has actively encouraged migration to Scotland through its Fresh Talent initiative. This was partly born from fears that a shrinking population in Scotland would hinder its economic competitiveness.

During the two years from June 2004, an estimated 32,000 people from Eastern Europe came to live and work in Scotland, 20,000 of whom were Poles. For context, in the 2001 census, the White Other group – within which many of these new migrants are likely to belong – accounted for just 78,000 people in the whole of Scotland. Within this total are small numbers of American- and Dutch-born residents; 800 people from the Netherlands alone live in the Aberdeen area, where the Dutch oil company Shell operates a refinery.

Given its close proximity to Ireland, it is not surprising that Scotland has a relatively large Irish population. Nearly 50,000 people identified this as their ethnic origin in the 2001 census. In Glasgow, which is the city physically closest to the Irish mainland, Irish people make up 2 per cent of the local population.

Aside from the Other White British, the next largest ethnic minority group in Scotland is Asian. Although Asian residents make up barely more than 1 per cent of the population as a whole (55,000 people), in some inner-city areas they are highly concentrated. In parts of central Glasgow, such as Pollokshields, as much as 40 per cent of the local population are of Pakistani origin. This city has more than 15,000 Pakistani residents, very nearly half of all people from this group living in Scotland. Unlike in England, where Indians form the largest Asian sub-group, in Scotland it is Pakistanis who predominate, by nearly two to one.

Scotland has very few black residents; around 8,000, or 0.2 per cent of the population. Even where people from this group are most strongly concentrated (in Perth), they account for rather less than 0.5 per cent of the local population. Black Africans outnumber Black Caribbeans by almost three to one; in England, Black Caribbeans are slightly more populous than Black Africans. The Chinese population is twice as large as the black population, and proportionally almost the same as in England; only this and the White Irish group are proportionally similarly represented in the population of both countries.

6

Valuing ethnic diversity and facilitating inclusion

Noticing ethnic diversity is not a sin, nor is it discriminatory. For many people the idea that we should say that we notice that someone is a different colour is at best embarrassing and at worst discrimination of the most serious kind. The belief and thinking that often underpins the embarrassment and the assumption that 'noticing' is discriminatory is that difference/diversity equals deficit. It is thinking that says, to be 'different from me' is to be somehow 'less than me'. As long as there is an underlying belief that difference equates to deficit then valuing ethnic diversity will be difficult, if not impossible, for anyone subscribing to that belief.

Becoming visible to minority ethnic communities

Most churches need to think about their visibility in the community generally, never mind in the minority ethnic community in particular. How the church is perceived by those both outside and inside the church is important. However, in the context of minority ethnic mission, getting to the stage where the church is perceived at all by members of minority ethnic communities is a necessary and critical first step. The fact that the church building may be in a prominent position and even recognized and used as a landmark does not mean that there is a conscious understanding among members of minority ethnic communities that it is a place of Christian worship and fellowship and that it is a place that is open to them.

Some years ago I came across a phrase that I like to use from time to time: 'the lights are on, but there's no one home'. I use it to describe situations where individuals are present, clearly awake but blissfully unaware of what is going on round about them. If they continue in that state they get ignored and passed over. Other people simply assume that they have no interest in being involved in what is going on.

It could well be that the church, your church, is perceived in the self-same way by members of minority ethnic communities. 'The lights are on, but there is no one home.' It could well be being assumed that the church has no interest in being involved in the community and has no awareness about the things people are interested in or concerned about.

Invisibility used to be the province of most, if not all, minority ethnic people. Being overlooked while queuing in the shops used to be a daily occurrence for early migrants. These days it is possibly the case that it is your church that has become invisible to members of these very same communities for whom invisibility had almost become a way of life.

Becoming visible will mean increasing your awareness of community interests and concerns, demonstrating involvement in the community, and most importantly going out and listening to the communities. Getting good at listening to the communities is vital. The way we listen and what we listen for affects what we hear, therefore the way we listen will determine how well we listen.

Sometimes we are listening simply for an opportunity to speak; we have our agenda, we are clear about what we need to tell the community, or what we want to ask the community about. The whole of our listening is focused on spotting that opportunity to speak. Sometimes we listen in order to correct the speaker; we listen for the inaccuracies in their assumptions about who we are and what we stand for. We are anxious that they should understand us. When we listen in these ways we are unlikely to hear the communities' concerns and interests.

Getting good at listening means listening to understand; listening for a chance to support; listening for opportunities to empathize.

Ten basic tips for good listening

1. Look at the speaker – listen with your eyes as well as your ears.
2. Stay alert and attentive – screen out distractions.
3. Manage your mind – keep it open, suspend judgements.
4. Focus on key words and issues – try to picture what the speaker is saying.
5. Pay attention to signals other than the words – tone, facial expressions, gestures, posture.
6. Give the speaker regular feedback – nodding, reflecting understanding.
7. Consciously spend more time listening than speaking – this may seem an obvious point, however . . .
8. Ask questions for clarification and understanding.
9. Don't interrupt and don't impose your 'solutions'.
10. When in doubt about whether to listen or speak, keep listening!

These tips can be used equally well with organizations and with individuals. Visualize a minority ethnic community organization you want to be more visible to and, using the tips, list the things you could do and things that you already do, but which you could do differently.

Distinguishing equality, diversity and inclusion

Equal opportunity and diversity are not the same things. Many people use the terms as though they were interchangeable, thinking that 'diversity is what we call it now'. This is a serious error with important implications for the decisions a church might take in addressing ethnic diversity and equality.

Equal opportunity

Equal opportunity is about:

- tackling irrelevant discrimination and dealing with inequality;
- fairness, decency, respect and high standards of behaviour between individuals and groups;

- demonstrating the will to extend yourself for the purpose of nurturing someone else's growth and development.

In corporate terms, equal opportunity is a concept underpinned by legislation. It requires organizations to provide relevant and appropriate access for the participation, development and advancement of all individuals and groups. In turn, equal opportunity requires individuals and groups to conduct themselves in particular ways when interacting with others.

From an individual perspective, experiencing equal opportunity is having access to relevant services, real choice to participate in, and/or contribute to, activities or processes and believing that you are being treated appropriately in relation to your ability and circumstances.

Diversity

Diversity, on the other hand, is a given. It is not an option or something to decide to have or not to have. Where there are two or more people, you have diversity. Diversity is difference and we are all different from each other.

Our differences include:

- family background
- age
- ethnic origin
- gender
- physical dis/abilities and qualities and appearance
- nationality
- sexual orientation
- educational background
- learning ability
- marital status
- parental status
- religious beliefs
- life and work and experience
- the other experiences that have touched our lives or influenced our thinking.

Differences between us give us a unique range of attributes and characteristics and a distinctive view of the world.

Similarity

There is a natural human tendency to gravitate towards people who are similar. Most of us feel more comfortable, at ease, secure and more able to 'be ourselves' when we are with people like ourselves. For us, similarity is generally the order of the day. The old saying 'birds of a feather flock together' resonates strongly in most social settings and even in churches.

Although most organizations say that they want individuals to bring different and innovative approaches, in practice they operate on the basis that difference is of little or no value and similarity is of great importance. This is usually not conscious or deliberate, but unless deliberate and positive action is taken to recognize, acknowledge and promote the value of diversity, then the old order will prevail.

Uniformity holds churches together, but there needs to be sufficient diversity to stop them dying. For any system to survive there needs to be sufficient difference within it to cope with environmental change, among many other things. Difference adds value.

Our similarities hold us together, and help us to work together. Our differences not only keep our churches alive, our differences make our work more effective and efficient. Imagine your church with an 'Antioch' leadership team (not all men though) that reflected the diversity of the communities it was serving. Would it make a difference to the effectiveness of the church in that place?

Similarity and diversity are like two sides of the same coin. Both sides are necessary if the coin is to be of value. In the case of similarity and diversity, the more tightly bound they are, the greater the value of the 'currency'. Pulling them apart simply devalues the 'currency'. Churches need to help their people to understand and value those things that they hold in common and that bind them together. This should be very straightforward, since we have creeds, doctrines and so on. At the same time we need to recognize, acknowledge and utilize the differences our people bring and consistently encourage them to display and utilize those differences for the benefit of the whole church community.

Managing inclusion

It has become fashionable in recent years to talk about managing diversity. I fully understand why and how this has come about. Indeed in many ways I have to share some responsibility for the phrase being in common use in equal opportunity and diversity circles. In April 1991, in London, I organized what I believe was the first 'Managing Diversity' conference for business executives and senior managers. Even with hindsight, I still believe it was probably an appropriate focus and language at that time. However, since then my thinking has changed.

For many people, the term 'managing diversity' usually conjures up an image of difficulties and problems that must be dealt with. Courses, programmes and policies called 'Managing Diversity' therefore are often perceived, and frequently subconsciously received by the participants, as addressing the 'problems' of, and not the opportunities offered through, diversity. This is not helpful, to say the least.

Managing diversity is impossible. Diversity is like time in this respect – we have it whether we like it or not. We can use it well, or abuse it, make the most of it or waste it; what we cannot do is 'manage' it. When it comes to using our time more productively what we try to do is to manage ourselves better.

When our focus is diversity, and our intention is to increase the benefits we derive from diversity, the action we have to take is to 'manage inclusion'.

Managing inclusion: assumptions

The need to 'manage inclusion' and its centrality in terms of valuing diversity is based on a number of simple assumptions.

- Most leadership teams or other groups in churches have members who are not fully engaged in the work of the team and, as a consequence, the team operates at less than 100 per cent, sometimes a lot less than 100 per cent.

- It is often the case that the team members who are not fully engaged in the work do not feel fully included in the team.
- The individuals who feel excluded often include a disproportionately high percentage of members of minority ethnic groups.
- There are a large number of people in organizations who do not feel they are included in, and therefore do not fully contribute to, the work of their teams.

If you are part of the leadership team or lead a group within the church, become expert at actively and deliberately treating people well. Make sure they are aware of what membership of the group means, that you are committed to their involvement in the group and intend to value their contribution to the group.

- Invest time in getting to know them – their areas of experience, knowledge, skills and concerns.
- Deliberately find ways of using the experience, knowledge or skills that they bring.
- Encourage and praise their contributions to the group and be detailed and specific about what they did and what made it so good in your eyes.
- Facilitate access to informal and formal development opportunities, training, coaching, mentoring and work-shadowing to support and encourage personal development.
- Expect members of the group to develop and perform in different ways and encourage them to support each other's diversity.

7

Developing a more diverse membership

We are going to consider 5 Cs under this heading: commitment, challenge, culture, community and contribution.

Commitment

It is vital that the Church is committed to being more ethnically diverse. If there is no real commitment, then the policies and day-to-day priorities of the Church will not reflect, or even take account of, the diversity objectives. Commitment needs to be seen in the leadership team (though it doesn't necessarily have to have started there).

Challenge

The vast majority of churches, even 'black majority churches', face enormous challenges when it comes to creating and maintaining an ethnically diverse membership. I believe this happens because how our churches look, or are perceived to be, will often dictate who feels able to come through the door. If this is true, then no matter what the current ethnic make-up of your church, if you want it to be more ethnically diverse than it is you will need to be very proactive and do more than pray.

It will be necessary to engage in outreach activities to the 'missing groups'. What you are about to read might betray my lack of faith, but I do not believe that the 'missing groups' will find their way to you simply because you pray about it and have 'All Welcome' on the noticeboard outside the church.

There is a joke about a Christian who went to church every Sunday and consistently prayed that this week he would win the lottery. Nothing happened, no answer from God and week after week he failed to win. In frustration he cried out to God complaining that he had always lived a good life, had supported the church through tithing, looked after his family, given to charity, been kind to neighbours, had never before asked God for anything for himself and now that he was asking for this relatively small thing he wasn't even getting an answer. After a while he stopped his complaining just in time to hear a loud voice say, 'Do me a favour and buy a ticket.'

We need to take action if we want things to be different. The temple walls would never have been rebuilt if Nehemiah had failed to 'buy a ticket' and work in partnership with God (Neh. 1).

There are five interrelated steps to take in order to attract individuals from the 'missing groups':

1 Assess the present situation and determine the priorities for action.
2 Decide the specific aims of the outreach programme.
3 Find out as much as you can about the target group(s).
4 Develop and implement an action plan.
5 Review progress and revise your plan as necessary.

Step 1: Assess the present situation

Gather necessary background information:

- Which minority ethnic communities are there in your 'parish'?
- What proportion of the overall population do they represent?
- What proportion of the current membership are of minority ethnic origin?
- Is the proportion of minority ethnic members reflected in church leadership?
- Is the proportion of minority ethnic members reflected in paid roles?

- What proportion of visitors are of minority ethnic origin?
- What proportion of newcomers are of minority ethnic origin?
- What proportion of recent leavers were of minority ethnic origin?

Identify areas of concern or under-representation. Analysing the data gathered in answer to the questions in the previous section will enable you to identify the areas you would want to focus on. These might include:

- minority ethnic 'under-representation' in the membership generally;
- minority ethnic 'under-representation' in particular areas of church activity;
- a low level of minority ethnic visitors;
- a lower proportion of minority ethnic visitors becoming newcomers or members.

Step 2: Decide specific aims

The overall aims for any minority ethnic outreach programme must take account of the wider church mission and specific aims or objectives, and will clearly need to reflect the needs of the local community and the local environment. Specific aims might include:

- ensuring that the relevant minority ethnic communities understand that the church is committed to being open to everyone and serving the entire community;
- ensuring that influential members of the relevant minority ethnic communities are aware of the church and its commitments;
- building long-term links with organizations and institutions capable of informing or influencing members of minority ethnic communities;
- ensuring that existing minority ethnic members are fully engaged in church life and that the leadership team reflects the make-up of the church.

Step 3: Finding out about the target group

- Consult the 2001 census data.
- Talk to the Commission for Equality and Human Rights and/ or the local Race Equality Council.
- Talk to anyone you know who belongs to or has links with the target group. There may already be people in the congregation or connected to a group run by the church.
- Approach relevant cultural and community centres.

The more you know and are seen to know about the target group, in terms of cultures, priorities, preferences etc., the more accurately you will be able to target your outreach activities. You will also be demonstrating your commitment to involving different communities in the life of the church by the very act of researching the relevant group.

Step 4: The action plan

Clearly the shape and content of the plan will depend on the outcome of Steps 1, 2 and 3, the resources allocated and your judgement about the church's profile.

The profile of your church in the community is important when considering an outreach programme and it is a key element in its own right.

- Does the church have any kind of profile within the target community?
- If so, how is it perceived?
- If their perception is different from your reality, what action will you take?

Whatever your approach, your action plan might include all or a combination of the following:

Building links with minority ethnic communities generally

- Develop relationships with the leadership of key organizations. This will take time and would be best done by assigning different individuals to specific organizations.

- Ask for their help with the day-to-day activities that make up church life.
- Invite representatives of key organizations to visit your church; you could add 'community presentations' to the list of occasional church activities.
- Offer to provide speakers for meetings of relevant community organizations. Utilizing the experience, skills, expertise and interests of church members could well provide coverage for a wide range of subject areas that might be attractive and interesting to community organizations.
- Organize open days and social events.
- Produce information in the relevant 'mother tongue' – seek advice about levels of literacy in the relevant mother tongue because, as with any language, fluency does not necessarily mean literacy.
- Use the minority ethnic media and relevant community news sheets and noticeboards – send them your press releases, notices and invitations unless they tell you not to (but even that could generate a useful dialogue).
- Develop relationships with schools, colleges, careers advisors, youth clubs etc. to make them aware of your ambitions.

Informing minority ethnic communities of specific vacancies

- From time to time paid and unpaid positions will need to be filled in the church. Make sure that you send information about vacancies to the key organizations.
- Develop a database of influential individuals and keep them regularly informed.
- Communicate directly with existing employees.
- Use specialist recruitment agencies when large numbers of vacancies occur.
- Advertise in the minority ethnic media.

Step 5: Review progress

This is best done on a regular basis so that actions can be adjusted in the light of experience. Reviewing on a quarterly basis is recommended.

- Assess outcomes against the original objectives.
- Identify any unplanned and/or unexpected consequences and impact.
- Talk to those who had been consulted in Steps 1 to 4.
- Revise actions as necessary.

Alligators in the lobby

Do would-be visitors find it hard to cross the threshold? Have you ever heard someone in your church say, 'I am so glad I came, but it took me several attempts to actually walk through the door'? If would-be visitors think you've got 'alligators in the lobby' they won't cross it, not even if they are really interested in what's on offer. I don't suppose there are that many welcome teams that are snappy or really bite, but our would-be visitors don't necessarily know that. Take steps to actively address the perceptions of those you are wanting to reach out to and connect with. Don't wait for them to somehow discover that the alligators aren't real.

Culture

The culture of the church is a key issue in determining whether people, especially people who are different from the majority, stay beyond their initial visit. Charles Handy defines culture simply as 'the way we do things around here'.

The *things* being distinguished in this phrase could refer to your church as opposed to the church down the road; your denomination as opposed to the others; your religion as opposed to others; your town or county or country as opposed to theirs; people who look like you as opposed to those who look different, and so on. How established church members understand and deal with the implication of culture – 'the way we do things around here' – on a day-to-day basis is critically important when it comes to newcomers having a sense of belonging.

I can hear people speaking Handy's definition in a number of different and unconsciously unhelpful ways.

- '*This* is the way we do things around here' – perhaps said while demonstrating something to a newcomer who would be left in no doubt as to what was expected from her or him.
- 'This is the way *we* do things around here' – the hearer could be excused for believing that they have not yet become part of the 'we'.
- 'This is the way we do things around *here*' – the subtext for this emphasis is that no matter how things were done around 'there', wherever you are from, now that you are 'here' you will do it this way – if you want to belong!

This is not straightforward territory because the vast majority of people want to belong, want to understand 'how to do things around *here*' and are anxious not to offend. However, the way in which we introduce people to the culture of our church is vital. Offering to share, guide, answer questions is a much more inclusive approach than 'telling'.

It is impossible to overemphasize the fact that the way newcomers experience the culture of the church will be a significant, if not the significant, factor in determining whether or not they join the fellowship; and if they do decide to join, the length of time it takes for them to have a real sense of belonging.

There are four aspects of a church's culture – way of being/doing things – that I think are worth stressing at this point. They are clarity, congruence, consistency and contribution.

Clarity

Clarity is important for everyone in a church, but it is vital for those who might not yet feel that they are accepted or that they fully belong or are fully part of the membership. Ideally the culture of the church should be one that enables everyone to understand fully the difference between the beliefs and doctrines to which you must sign up if you want to be a member and the way things are done because that's how it suits us or because no one has ever thought about it being different. This is not to say that every newcomer will want to change things. The chances are that a church will be attractive to particular individuals precisely because of the way some things are done. Nevertheless, clarity in this area is important and the mere process of thinking about the distinctions between beliefs and doctrine and, let's call them, the traditional practices, could be a way of revitalizing the church to become more responsive and relevant to contemporary society and the diverse communities in which the church is placed.

Congruence

Congruence is about the church leadership 'walking the talk'. Do those with authority, responsibility and influence live up to the stated policies and priorities when it comes to minority ethnic mission? Is there congruence between what they say and what they do, and between their public statements in church and private beliefs and behaviours? Do those with whom they work in the church experience their differences being valued?

Consistency

Consistency can be a decisive factor for a newcomer trying to determine whether the church is going to value them. Does the sense of being wanted last beyond the first worship service and social event? Does the good-quality treatment and warmth of the fellowship extend beyond those in their 'pew'? Whether people stay or go will be determined by how valued they feel – whether they have a sense of belonging. The way newcomers experience the culture, 'the way we do things around here', will speak far more loudly than the sermons or church rules and regulations. So, the extent to which your church's culture is one that consistently values ethnic diversity will be vital.

Community

Creating a sense of community, of belonging, within the church is an important way of maintaining the membership on the basis that people *want* to stay, as opposed to people feeling that they have nowhere else to go. Actively facilitating access to all aspects of church life is the key to developing and maintaining a good sense of community. All members should feel that they have good access to:

- relevant information;
- support networks/fellowship groups and activities;
- discipleship and other learning and development programmes;
- opportunities for taking on responsibility and leadership within the church.

Contribution

Most of us want to feel that we contribute to society generally. We also want to contribute in our place of worship. We feel good when our contributions make a difference and add value to the whole. I believe this is a normal human emotion. As a key part of any minority ethnic mission strategy, churches need actively to seek contributions by:

- identifying and utilizing experience, knowledge and skills unique to individual members;
- involving all members when discussing and developing new ideas, approaches, activities and priorities;
- encouraging all church leaders to seek feedback from their groups or team members;
- encouraging members to bring new ideas and approaches to group team meetings;
- publicly acknowledging people's contributions, especially those that are behind the scenes and/or often regarded as mundane.

Dealing with blockages

Stereotyping

Stereotyping is seeing an individual in a particular way, or making an assumption about an individual because of the perceptions we have about a group to which we believe that individual belongs. It happens all the time everywhere.

Stereotyping individuals, or groups of individuals, is very prevalent in all societies. It may be conscious or unconscious, but either way it underlies much of the negative treatment that keeps people from feeling that they truly belong. It is important to get to know people individually instead of making judgements or assumptions about who they are.

Stereotyping someone based on perceptions about the group to which they belong can be damaging and unfair to that person. It is important that we pay attention to any tendencies we may have towards stereotyping others as it can lead to unfair treatment.

Many stereotypes suggest that some groups are lazy, or they're never on time, or they don't have a particular set of skills or attributes, or they can't do this or that particular thing. Individuals associated with such groups may find themselves labelled as 'less able', or 'less worthy'. The leadership can then very easily feel that they need not take any action to facilitate their greater involvement or encourage them to participate at a particular level because 'We all know they don't have the ability, don't we?'

Stereotypes may be conscious or unconscious. When they are unconscious, they shape our behaviour even though we're unaware of the influence. Stereotypical judgements about intelligence and emotional reactions to differences are pervasive in our society (and most other societies, too). They have permeated our beliefs and shaped the way we behave towards one another.

Our failure to recognize when we are stereotyping and our lack of awareness of the implications are the main issues. Every time we think we know all about someone because 'We worked with lots of people "like them" in Africa/India' or 'We used to have a couple like them in the church', we fool ourselves.

Every time we catch ourselves stereotyping but think it's all right because it's a positive stereotype, we delude ourselves. So-called positive stereotypes are potentially even more dangerous than negative stereotypes. It works like this: we ascribe a positive characteristic to a particular group, we stereotype. When we meet people from that group we expect them to live up to our stereotype; if they don't and are only as good at that particular thing as people not from their group or background, we note that they have failed.

Stereotyping leads us to pre-judge individuals and pre-judgement may cause us to discriminate in relation to them. Understanding our own proneness to stereotype is vital if we are to get good at managing the inclusion of others.

It is important to understand that the stereotypes we hold about a group tell us absolutely nothing about a particular individual member of that group. At the same time, our ability to understand the stereotypes that are prevalent in society regarding different groups or communities provides us with some insight into what individual members of that group or community may be experiencing on a day-to-day basis. If you believe that you never stereotype, you might do well to ask someone you spend time with for some feedback!

Negative treatment

It will be obvious to all of us that when people are physically or verbally abused simply because of their ethnic origin they will feel excluded and subsequently feel less inclined to participate in church activities. Negative treatment comes in a variety of forms, however, and frequently the 'victim' doesn't even feel able to complain. People in this situation may be being ignored, or never asked about their work or their holiday. There may be frequent jokes about aspects of their culture or language or country of origin – though of course he or she will be assured that it's all in good fun and it's just friendly banter. I think of these things as low-level negative treatment.

Low-level negative treatment can be likened to the constant drip, drip, drip from a guttering with a hole in when it rains. Even the most aware church leaders are not always around 'when it's raining', and if they are around, they don't always notice. If they do notice, they don't always understand the potential impact of a little drip and that it could be a major problem. Even if they are conscious of the potential impact, they may well not feel equipped to intervene.

As we are all aware, however, if it is not dealt with, dripping water from the guttering will, over time, erode the concrete that it drips on to. In the same way, low-level negative treatment will eventually destroy people's self-esteem, sense of belonging and willingness to remain in the fellowship. Church leaders need to 'watch out for the drips' in the membership and ensure that they are dealt with promptly before erosion sets in.

Drips need to be taken to one side and helped to understand what the impact of their behaviour could be over time. They will particularly need help to see that just because the target of their 'negative treatment' seems to be 'enjoying the joke', 'taking it in the spirit that it's meant', 'laughing along with everyone else', it is not an indication that their behaviour is helpful, supportive or having a positive impact on the self-esteem of the 'target'.

8

A strategy for action

Many churches operate on the basis that their doors are open to all and that those who need them will find their way to them.

The most effective and important thing that can be done to increase the likelihood that minority ethnic people will 'find their way to you' is to engage in dialogue with them. This needs to be more than a survey and should be seen as an ongoing process rather than a one-off activity.

Churches with a congregation that reflects the communities they serve are clearly in a good position to be proactive when it comes to meeting the diverse needs of those communities. However, they need to demonstrate that they value the diversity of their congregation if they are to be successful in engaging them in any effort to access hard-to-reach communities.

Requirements

If a church is to progress in terms of ethnic diversity there needs to be a vision, personal commitment, a coherent strategy and relevant organizational activity and processes.

Someone with seniority and influence in the leadership of the church must be committed to recognizing and getting value from ethnic diversity. Unless there is at least one person with a strong commitment to the vision, the chances are there will be little or no progress and any progress that is made will be difficult, if not impossible, to sustain.

Vision

The vision for a multi-ethnic church or multi-ethnic mission must answer the question, 'What will it look like when it's done?'

The ethnic diversity mission must be an integral part of the broader church vision. If this is not so then there is little chance of it being accomplished. If it is clear that the vision or mission of the church is not congruent with the concept of a church reflecting the diversity of the community then something will have to be changed or abandoned, because the two positions are incompatible.

Ideally, the whole church will share the ethnic diversity vision and be committed to it being achieved.

Once there is a vision, which is best able to be conveyed in two or three sentences, then it is possible to develop an effective strategy designed to move the organization towards the vision. Appropriate implementation plans then need to be developed to achieve the strategic priorities.

Strategy

There must be a coherent strategy with clearly defined implementation plans, which when accomplished will move the church closer to the long-term goal. The strategy is simply the approach that will be taken, the five or six broad areas that will be addressed, in order to move towards the vision. Having a strategy enables you to determine where to invest your resources and prevents you going off in several different, possibly conflicting, directions all at once.

When it comes to the diversity agenda, experience suggests that there are a number of key elements that need to be included in a diversity strategy no matter what the vision. Image, leadership and accountability are vital components. Beyond that, the other strategic priorities could include communication, but identifying the other relevant components does depend on the vision and context.

Addressing the issues of image, leadership and accountability is vital if there is to be real progress on this agenda.

When it comes to multi-ethnic mission, how the church is seen by those both outside and inside, the nature and consistency of the leadership and the extent to which the leadership is accountable and holds others to account, will determine the quality of the relationships within the church and between the church and others with whom it relates.

Communication

Many organizations committed to equality and valuing diversity have failed to make the headway they should have because they did not have a communication strategy. Good communication is important generally, but when it comes to addressing this issue, it becomes vital because everybody believes they have something at stake, and often lots of people believe they are going to lose out.

Making it work

An effective strategy needs to be overseen by the leadership team and led by someone with influence and authority in the church. The leadership team should meet say, four times each year specifically to address the strategy. One of its purposes must be to keep the issues on everybody else's agenda. Quarterly meetings with progress reports from all the key players is one way of doing this.

Specific implementation plans designed to achieve the strategic priorities should be related to, and be the responsibility of the department or group or team into whose area they fall – for instance, worship group, house groups, community outreach etc. They should cover a period of at least twelve months and be reviewed quarterly by the leadership team.

If new perceptions, policies, priorities or practices regarding ethnic diversity and mission are to be self-sustaining (and that should surely be the aim), then the strategy must insure that they are integrated into those existing priorities and practices that are seen as critical to the church's success. It is therefore vital that new ways of thinking and being in the area of ethnic diversity and mission become part of, and not held apart from, the culture of the church.

The 5 Ds – desire, definition, decision, determination and discipline – can help churches and church organizations to get a vision and strategy in place, get into action and stay on track.

Desire

Does the church, or at least the part of the church that makes and drives the policy priorities, have a desire to address the minority ethnic mission? Is there a pull towards the benefits of ethnic diversity and an understanding of the importance of managing the inclusion of individuals from minority ethnic groups? Or is it simply a push away from the fear of being thought of as discriminating against certain groups or individuals?

Try answering the following questions with yes or no:

- Do you believe that a more ethnically diverse congregation means adding value to worship services?
- Do you believe that a more ethnically diverse congregation means adding potential to the church fellowship?
- Do you believe that a more ethnically diverse church membership means greater potential for serving the community?
- Do you want to see more ethnic diversity in the leadership team?
- Do you expect all church members to do things differently?
- Do you believe that it is necessary actively to target communities that are hard to reach?

The more times you answer yes, the stronger your desire.

Definition

Many churches try to become active around the ethnic diversity agenda without ever properly defining what they mean and getting clear about what it is they want to achieve. The fact is, the clearer you can be about your goal, the greater your chances of staying on track. This is true no matter what you are wanting to achieve or the area of activity you are concerned about. It is a vital ingredient when it comes to seeking value from ethnic diversity.

To define clearly what you want to achieve means taking yourself to the point in time when what you want to achieve has been achieved and describing what it looks like, feels like, smells like. It is best described as visualization – the creation of a strong mental image.

So, describe the vision. What will it look like when it's done?

Decision

It might seem odd to have 'decision' spelt out but sometimes churches never get around to making decisions to take action about the things that they discuss. Issues associated with ethnic diversity are often left in the 'no decision taken' basket.

It is important that a decision is taken to seek to realize the vision rather than, as is often the case, simply to agree that ethnic diversity is rather a good idea. The relevant body needs to decide that action will be taken to move towards the vision. They need also to set specific goals, decide who will be responsible for ensuring the goals are achieved and who they are to be accountable to for achieving the goals.

Determination

Churches setting out to reach minority ethnic communities need to see it as a long-term process. This is not to say that there may not be 'quick wins' and benefits that show up in the short term. However, accessing hard-to-reach groups and increasing the diversity of the leadership team will require that you take a longer-term view.

The team driving the process will also be subject to criticism – more or less sustained, and from two opposite poles. First, you will be criticized for not moving quickly enough. Your 'slow pace' will be absolute proof of your total lack of commitment. You need to stay consistent at this stage and restate your commitment to the vision – 'What will it look like when it's done?' – and demonstrate that you are on track in relation to the action plan, if in fact you are. Or explain why there is slippage against the plans, if there is, and what action will be taken, and when, to get back on track. Whether on track or not, tell the criticizers that you would value their help and ask them how or what they will contribute to achieving the implementation plan and/or how they think the plan could be improved.

Second, you will be criticized for 'going over the top', 'discriminating against our own people', 'wasting resources', being 'politically correct', and so on. You should ask this group to consider whether it makes sense to take specific action to engage with and actively offer the church to all people in the parish or catchment area. They will hopefully say yes. This will set you up to explain what your church is trying to achieve through its minority ethnic mission work. You could also remind them of the ethnic diversity of the early church (Acts 13.1), and Jesus' interaction with the woman at the well (John 4.7).

Discipline

A disciplined approach is called for if progress is to be made and sustained. The area where indiscipline sets in soonest is the review meeting. The regular (monthly) meeting to review progress, acknowledge achievements and reset short-term goals (as necessary) is vital to maintain momentum, yet it is often the first casualty of an undisciplined approach. This is usually described in terms of busy diaries and a very full church programme.

Staying in communication with the different groups, both inside and outside the church, who were involved in any research or planning as the strategy was being formulated is important but requires discipline. It is easy for this apparently peripheral activity to be overlooked because you are too busy 'doing the work' to talk to others about it. The communication plan should be seen as part and parcel of the work and have the same status as other areas of activity.

Staying focused

A top priority for somebody with seniority and influence

There has to be someone taking responsibility for ensuring that something happens. If there isn't, then things grind to a halt, if indeed they ever get started. The person who has responsibility needs also to have it as a priority.

Sadly, when the ethnic diversity agenda is being addressed, it is not always the case that someone with seniority and influence has minority ethnic mission as one of their top priorities. It is always the case, however, that success is far more likely if this level of prioritizing and accountability can be achieved.

Focus on what you want

When it comes to minority ethnic and equality issues generally, there is a strong tendency for churches to focus most, if not all, of their energy on what they are wanting to avoid rather than what they want to achieve. This leads to policies and programmes being created around avoiding unlawful and unnecessary discrimination and dealing with any apparent unhelpful or inappropriate behaviour.

There is nothing inherently wrong with wanting to avoid those things, indeed they do need to be tackled, but the best way to do this is to stay focused on what you want – active inclusion and engagement in the church fellowship at all levels. However you articulate it, the key is to accentuate the positive things you want rather than dwell on the negative things you are trying to avoid. We are all far more attracted to individuals and groups whom we see as striving to achieve something as opposed to those individuals and groups we perceive to be constantly moaning about various things.

Be prepared to do things differently

One thing is certain if your church is to achieve its aspirations regarding minority ethnic mission: you will have to do things differently. This may come as a shock, but it stands to reason that if you haven't got what you want from what you have been doing, then you need to do things differently or, heaven forbid, do different things. It is surprising how relatively easy it is to set objectives, decide that things need to be different and then discover that you can't identify anything that you think needs to be changed or done differently. Don't forget that there are many minority ethnic community organizations that could be a rich source of information and support.

Having said that, it is sometimes the case that some of the very people you are trying to 'include' are unsure what could be done differently, and even when asked directly may not have an immediate answer. You need consistently to assure them of your preparedness to do things differently and take every opportunity to encourage them to come back to you every time they discover something, however small, that they think could be done differently to help the church to make progress towards its minority ethnic mission objectives. When this happens, take action as quickly as possible. Even if it doesn't work out as planned, it's vital to demonstrate that you are serious about wanting their contribution.

Make sure the music fits the words

Congruence is the key. There needs to be consistency between the church's policies, priorities and practice. This is particularly important for church leaders at every level. Every time anyone in a leadership role fails to practise what the church preaches in respect of minority ethnic mission, there will be dissonance and discord, and those concerned with that particular aspect of church life 'hear' that the music does not fit the words.

Senior leaders in particular need to ensure that they 'walk the talk' because they will come in for close scrutiny in respect of the minority ethnic mission. For large churches and church headquarters' organizations, how leaders are seen to behave in their private offices – how they speak about the minority ethnic staff, what they say about press articles addressing minority ethnic issues etc. – will become common knowledge no matter how 'private' they thought it was. The extent to which senior leaders are perceived to be 'walking the talk' or not 'walking the talk' will be an important, even if unfair, sign of the extent to which the church is serious about and committed to achieving its minority ethnic mission objectives.

Make minority ethnic mission objectives count in the annual appraisal

Where the church has employees who are subject to annual appraisals it is important that minority ethnic mission is taken account of in the process. The first part of this is of course to make sure that all employees have relevant minority ethnic mission objectives.

The objectives need to be relevant to the particular role and must be recognized and acknowledged as such by the appraiser. Whether the objective is achieved or not achieved must be noted and be clearly seen to make a difference to the marking and/or commentary and/or learning and development plan that follows the appraisal.

Recognize that *you* have to do something

Whoever you are and whatever your role in the church, you have to do something if you want things on the ethnic diversity agenda to be different. You cannot be a passenger and simply hope that someone else will do whatever needs to be done. You have to decide to be that someone if you want things to change. The very least you can do is to get this book into the hands of whoever you think has the authority and/or the commitment and/or the influence to make things happen.

Whatever you do, don't just read about it – *take some action.*

9

Leading multi-ethnic mission

If you are taking a lead when it comes to multi-ethnic mission it might very well be useful to pay attention to the following areas of action:

- informing and educating
- supporting leaders
- facilitating access
- evaluating outcomes
- providing regular feedback.

Informing and educating

The fact that addressing the ethnic diversity agenda has a direct relevance to the church and its mission won't necessarily be obvious to all the members of the church. This could well include some of those in relatively senior and influential positions or occupying formal leadership roles.

In championing minority ethnic mission you may well need to go back to basics consistently with your brothers and sisters to help them see why it matters and why there will be a 'Kingdom cost' if we bury our heads.

Informing and educating is best done 'as and when' in response to comments or questions. You should also take opportunities to point out any minority ethnic mission implications or opportunities during discussions about other church issues.

Addressing questions and responding to opportunities in a direct, informative and supportive way is a powerful way to bring people on without them feeling that they have been 'got at' or lectured to.

Supporting leaders

A powerful way of supporting leaders is to help and mentor those in positions of responsibility and influence and those with formal leadership roles to build minority ethnic mission into their part of church life. Inviting them to address the following questions can be a helpful point of entry:

- Are there minority ethnic communities in our area that we are failing to reach and, if so, how much do we know about them?
- Are there any existing church members or staff who are connected with any of those minority ethnic communities?
- If yes, how involved are they in any efforts to reach others from those communities?
- If we don't have any church members or staff, should we be seeking to target our outreach activities?
- How could we better utilize the unique experience, knowledge and skills of existing church members or staff?

Facilitating access

House or fellowship groups or staff support groups are often established, or indeed form themselves, around different ethnic groups. Whether as small fellowship groups, study groups, social groups or congregations, groups made up largely or totally of people from the same ethnic background are not and should not be seen as a problem.

An important area to focus on if you are leading minority ethnic mission is to help the different groups to remain strongly connected to, and to tap into and be fully part of, the wider church fellowship, so they can be both sustained by and add value to the whole body of the Church.

Evaluating outcomes

In reviewing the church's business plan or equivalent document you should ask:

- To what extent was any account taken of multi-ethnic mission?
- If there were any multi-ethnic mission specific actions, how effective were they?
- Are the current priorities still the appropriate way to move towards the vision of the Kingdom now in the light of local demographics and any changed circumstances?

If your current monitoring processes are not sufficiently advanced to enable you to get answers to these questions, your task will be to put processes in place that will enable the three questions to be answered, in order to help the church to stay on track.

In the Salvation Army there is an 'annual census' in every corps taken on a Sunday in July. It covers age, gender and ethnic origin. This annual snapshot helps to give a feel of how things are at a particular point in time and is an important indicator of the trends.

Providing regular feedback

Keep the leadership team up to speed with what's going on with the minority ethnic mission agenda, whether they want to know or not! There will be many reasons cited as to why their agendas may not specifically address minority ethnic mission; the day-to-day demands of running the church; the fact that the leadership needs to concern itself with 'the whole Church', and so on. Take every opportunity to highlight the connections between the day-to-day agenda of general Kingdom-building and the minority ethnic mission. Focus the team on the need specifically to target minority ethnic communities if those who are part of or affiliated to those communities are to feel that the church is relevant to them.

Don't wait for someone else to ask, but report back, or ask others to report back, on a formal basis, say, quarterly.

10

Checklist for a multi-ethnic church

If there is to be change in a church, especially a busy one, then the area of change, the new or different things being introduced, must be strongly focused on by the leadership team. The checklist below provides a working framework to help the leadership team to develop and maintain focus.

1 Valuing ethnic diversity from the top.
2 Articulating the vision.
3 Awareness education.
4 Enlisting support at all levels.
5 Developing ethnic diversity in decision-making groups.
6 Encouraging social networks, fellowship and support groups.
7 Monitoring and evaluation.

A good way to get a feel for where your church is regarding the minority ethnic mission is to review the following questions:

1 Valuing diversity from the top

To what extent does the leadership team, or the most senior body in the organization, take responsibility for the vision of a multiethnic church?

____

____

How does the leadership demonstrate that it is an open and accessible church or organization, keen to reflect the ethnic diversity of the communities it serves and is consciously striving to utilize all available talent?

How does the most senior person ensure that all those with responsibility and those in formal leadership roles set personal diversity objectives and hold them to account?

To what extent does the annual planning process include minority ethnic mission priorities?

2 Articulating the vision

How and where are members of the leadership team and others with responsibility in the church articulating the minority ethnic mission priorities?

How is the vision for a multi-ethnic church reflected in the church's overall objectives and priorities?

How effective is the communication process in ensuring that all members are aware of the vision for a multi-ethnic church and the fact that they have a role to play in the vision being fulfilled?

3 Awareness education

How much access do church leaders and staff have to information and/or programmes to keep them up to date with equality legislation?

Are there any specific learning and development programmes or processes designed to inform and educate church leaders, members and staff about the issues associated with a multi-ethnic church?

To what extent do discipleship and other learning and development programmes reflect the church's minority ethnic mission aspirations?

4 Enlisting support at all levels

How committed are the leadership team, other church leaders, church staff and members to the vision of a multi-ethnic church, and what will be done to maintain their commitment?

Leadership team ____

____

Other church leaders ____________________________________

____

Church staff ____

____

Members ____

____

5 Developing ethnic diversity in decision-making groups

Most churches operate on the basis that decision-making, accountability, responsibility and hierarchy are inextricably linked even when the decision is taken by, or involves, a group rather than an individual.

This need not be the case, especially when a church is conscious that members of particular groups are 'underrepresented' in leadership and senior roles. Deciding to uncouple the decision-making process from the system of accountability could be extremely liberating. Deliberately creating and maintaining decision-making groups that reflect the ethnic diversity of the congregation would probably radically increase the creative potential of most churches.

The lines of accountability need not be changed and the relevant members of the hierarchy would still have to 'carry the can' and be accountable for the good governance of the church even though decisions were being taken by groups who were not made up entirely of people who were there because of their position in the hierarchy. It could even lead to decision-making groups made up of people who were more qualified to address the responsibilities of the relevant group if the membership of the group was not a direct consequence of holding a job or position in the church.

In which areas of your church's work could the ethnic diversity of the decision-making group be increased?

6 Encouraging social networks, fellowship and study groups

How does your church facilitate, encourage and involve social networks, fellowship and study groups?

How could the church increase their understanding of their vision of a multi-ethnic church?

How could their appreciation of the role and importance of the other social networks, fellowship and study groups be increased?

How could each network/group be more closely involved in developing plans to move the church towards its multi-ethnic vision?

____

____

7 Monitoring and evaluation

To what extent does the church have a framework for collecting, analysing and utilizing data regarding ethnic diversity issues relevant to the church?

____

____

How frequently do we review existing data-collecting processes and determine what needs to be dropped or changed and what else needs to be done?

____

____

How do we evaluate the effectiveness of our minority ethnic mission strategy?

____

____

11

Anti-discrimination legislation in the UK – an overview

This chapter is particularly important for those churches with staff teams and for those leaders who have recruitment and staff management responsibilities.

Definition of terms

The following terms and phrases feature in UK anti-discrimination legislation and may have slightly different meanings to those used in everyday language. Unless stated otherwise the meaning of the term is the same in whichever specific anti-discrimination legislation it is used.

Direct discrimination

Direct discrimination on the relevant grounds occurs where a person treats someone less favourably on those relevant grounds than he or she treats other people.

Indirect discrimination

Indirect unfair discrimination on the relevant grounds occurs when a requirement or condition is imposed which appears to apply equally to all groups but which is unfairly discriminatory in its effect on the relevant group. A condition or requirement would be unfairly discriminatory if:

- the proportion of the relevant group which could comply with it was considerably smaller than the proportion of the other group, *and*

- it could not be shown to be justifiable, irrespective of the group to which the person to whom it was applied belonged, *and*
- it was detrimental to an individual because he or she could not comply with it.

Harassment

Harassment refers to unwanted conduct that violates people's dignity or creates an intimidating, hostile, degrading, humiliating or offensive environment.

Victimization

Victimization describes treating people less favourably because of something they have done under, or in connection with, the legislation/regulations, for example making a formal complaint of discrimination or giving evidence in a tribunal case.

Positive action

The Sex Discrimination Act and Race Relations Act allow employers actively to encourage people from under-represented groups to apply for training and employment opportunities and to prepare them to compete on equal terms for jobs and promotion. This is called positive action. However, actual recruitment to all jobs must be strictly on merit.

Genuine occupational qualification/requirement

Discrimination on the grounds of age, disability, race or sex is not unlawful in circumstances where a genuine occupational qualification/requirement is established.

Disability Discrimination Act (DDA) 1995

The DDA defines a disabled person as someone with a physical or mental impairment which has a substantial and long-term (i.e. expected to last for 12 months) adverse effect on their ability to carry out normal, day-to-day activities. The disability could be physical, sensory or mental. It includes conditions which have

A brief history of anti-discrimination legislation

1944 & 1958	Disabled Persons (Employment) Act	3% quota scheme, disabled persons register and record-keeping to show compliance.
1957	Treaty of Rome	Unlawful to discriminate against EEC workers on grounds of nationality and citizenship. Men and women should receive equal pay for equal work.
1965	Race Relations Act	Unlawful to discriminate on grounds of colour, race, ethnic or national origins in 'places of public resort'.
1968	Race Relations Act	Extended the 1965 Act into employment, provision of services and housing provision.
1970	Equal Pay Act and Equal Pay Act Northern Ireland	Unlawful to discriminate between men and women with regards to pay and other contractual terms and conditions.
	Chronically Sick and Disabled Persons Act	Provision for physical access to public buildings, parking facilities, toilets and signs.
1975	Sex Discrimination Act	Direct and indirect discrimination introduced. Concept of Positive Action and Genuine Occupational Qualification established. Equal Opportunities Commission established.
1976	SDA – Northern Ireland Order	Broadly speaking as 1975 SDA above.
1976	Race Relations Act	Replaced the previous RRAs. Established the Commission for Racial Equality. As SDA above, direct and indirect discrimination introduced. Concept of Positive Action and Genuine Occupational Qualification established.
	Chronically Sick and Disabled Persons Act (Amendment) Act	1970 Act amended to cover places of employment.

a slight effect on day-to-day activities but which are expected to become substantial (e.g. HIV/AIDS). Severe disfigurement is also classed as a disability.

The DDA:

- gives disabled people rights in employment, goods and services, buying or renting land or property;
- requires schools, colleges and universities to provide information for disabled people;
- allows the Government to set minimum standards so that disabled people can use public transport more easily;
- created the National Disability Commission to advise on discrimination against disabled people.

It is unlawful for an employer to treat a disabled person less favourably than someone else because of her or his disability unless there is a good reason. This applies to all employment matters, including recruitment, training, promotion and dismissal.

There is a duty on employers to make 'reasonable adjustments' to working arrangements and the work environment for a person with a disability. In considering what is reasonable, employers are able to take into account how much any changes would cost and how much they would help. Employers are not expected to make any changes that would break health and safety laws. Failure by an employer to comply with the duty to make reasonable adjustments without justification also amounts to unfair discrimination.

Goods, Facilities, Services and Property

The DDA affects anyone who provides goods, facilities or services to members of the public whether paid or free.

It is unlawful to:

- refuse to serve someone who is disabled;
- offer a disabled person a service that is not as good as the service offered to other people;
- provide a service to a disabled person on terms that are different to the terms given to other people;

- run a service or provide goods or facilities in a way that makes it impossible or unreasonably difficult for a disabled person to use the service or goods.

People must provide equipment or other helpful items that will make it easier for disabled people to use their service. People must remove physical obstructions or provide other ways of letting disabled people use their services if it is reasonable to do so. Service providers cannot charge a disabled person more to meet the cost of making it easier for them to use their service.

Exemptions

It would not be against the law to refuse to provide a service to a disabled person or to provide it on different terms if:

- the health and safety of the disabled person or other people were in danger;
- the customer was not capable of understanding the terms of the contract;
- providing the service or the same standard of service would deny service to other customers.

Human Rights Act 2000

For public authorities, the Human Rights Act makes it a legal duty to act compatibly with the European Convention on Human Rights (ECHR). If a person's rights are harmed she or he can take the public authority to court in this country. Included among the Articles of the Human Rights Act are:

- the right to life;
- the prohibition of forced labour;
- the right to liberty and security;
- the right to respect for private and family life;
- freedom of thought, conscience and religion;
- freedom of expression, assembly and association;
- the right to marry;
- and the prohibition of discrimination.

Many everyday acts by public authorities touch Convention rights in one way or another. For example, Article 8, Rights to Respect for Private and Family Life, might be harmed by the disclosure of personal information. A ban on wearing certain types of clothing might interfere with someone's religious belief, as set out in Article 9. And restrictions on 'whistle-blowing' might breach the right of expression in Article 10.

The Convention rights are interpreted widely – and in the light of modern standards of social policy. Interference with some rights is allowed, but only if the public authority can show that it met strict tests. For example, the interference must be proportionate, fair and lawful.

The Employment Equality (Sexual Orientation) Regulations 2003 and The Employment Equality (Religion or Belief) Regulations 2003

These Regulations outlaw discrimination in employment and vocational training on the grounds of sexual orientation and religion or belief respectively. The Regulations implement strands of the European Employment Directive (Council Directive 2000/78/EC).

What do the 2003 Regulations outlaw?

- Direct discrimination – treating people less favourably than others on grounds of sexual orientation or religion or belief.
- Indirect discrimination – applying a provision, criterion or practice that disadvantages people of a particular sexual orientation or religion or belief and that is not justified as a proportionate means of achieving a legitimate aim.
- Harassment – unwanted conduct that violates people's dignity or creates an intimidating, hostile, degrading, humiliating or offensive environment.
- Victimization – treating people less favourably because of something they have done under or in connection with the Regulations, e.g. made a formal complaint of discrimination or given evidence in a tribunal case.

What grounds do the 2003 Regulations cover?

The Sexual Orientation Regulations apply to discrimination on grounds of orientation towards persons of the same sex (lesbians and gays), the opposite sex (heterosexuals) and the same and opposite sex (bisexuals). They cover discrimination on grounds of perceived as well as actual sexual orientation (i.e. assuming – correctly or incorrectly – that someone is lesbian, gay, heterosexual or bisexual). The Regulations also cover association, i.e. being discriminated against on grounds of the sexual orientation of those with whom you associate (for example, friends and/or family).

The Religion or Belief Regulations apply to discrimination on grounds of religion, religious belief or similar philosophical belief. They cover discrimination on grounds of perceived as well as actual religion or belief (i.e. assuming – correctly or incorrectly – that someone has a particular religion or belief). The Regulations also cover association, i.e. being discriminated against on grounds of the religion or belief of those with whom you associate (for example, friends and/or family).

What do the 2003 Regulations not cover?

The Sexual Orientation Regulations *do not* cover discrimination other than discrimination on grounds of people's (actual or perceived) sexual orientation.

The Religion or Belief Regulations *do not* protect against discrimination on grounds of belief not akin to a religion or similar philosophical belief, e.g. being a fanatical supporter of a particular football club, or being a supporter of a particular political party because of strongly held political views.

What aspects of employment do the 2003 Regulations cover?

The Regulations apply throughout the employment relationship: during the recruitment process, in the workplace, on dismissal and, in certain circumstances, after the employment has finished.

Who do the 2003 Regulations cover?

The Regulations protect the rights of *workers*. They apply to all employers and businesses whatever their size and whether in the public or private sector (including the police). They apply to recruitment, terms and conditions, pay, promotion, transfers and dismissals.

They protect *office-holders* appointed by the Government and other office-holders where they fall within the scope of the Directive (that is, if they are paid and are subject to some form of direction). This means clergy and judicial offices, for example, including magistrates and employment tribunal members.

There are, however, exemptions for Genuine Occupational Requirement where:

(a) the employment or office is for purposes of an organised religion;
(b) the employer applies a requirement related to sexual orientation –
  (i) so as to comply with the doctrines of the religion, or
  (ii) because of the nature of the employment and the context in which it is carried out, so as to avoid conflicting with the strongly held religious convictions of a significant number of the religion's followers; and
(c) either –
  (i) the person to whom that requirement is applied does not meet it, or
  (ii) the employer is not satisfied, and in all the circumstances it is reasonable for him not to be satisfied, that that person meets it.

This paragraph applies where an employer has an ethos based on religion or belief and, having regard to that ethos and to the nature of the employment or the context in which it is carried out –

(a) being of a particular religion or belief is a genuine occupational requirement for the job;
(b) it is proportionate to apply that requirement in the particular case; and

(c) either –
  (i) the person to whom that requirement is applied does not meet it, or
  (ii) the employer is not satisfied, and in all the circumstances it is reasonable for him not to be satisfied, that that person meets it.

The Employment Equality (Age) Regulations 2006

These Regulations outlaw discrimination in employment and vocational training on the grounds of age. The Regulations implement strands of the European Employment Directive (Council Directive 2000/78/EC).

What do the 2006 Regulations outlaw?

The regulations make it unlawful on the grounds of age to:

- discriminate directly against anyone – that is, to treat them less favourably than others because of their age unless objectively justified;
- discriminate indirectly against anyone – that is, to apply a criterion, provision or practice which disadvantages people of a particular age unless it can be objectively justified;
- subject someone to harassment. Harassment is unwanted conduct that violates a person's dignity or creates an intimidating, hostile, degrading, humiliating or offensive environment for him or her having regard to all the circumstances including the perception of the victim;
- victimize someone because they have made or intend to make a complaint or allegation or have given or intend to give evidence in relation to a complaint of discrimination on grounds of age;
- discriminate against someone, in certain circumstances, after the working relationship has ended.

Who do the 2006 Regulations cover?

These regulations apply to all employers, private and public sector vocational training providers, trade unions, professional organizations, employer organizations and trustees and managers of occupational pension schemes. In this context an employer is anyone who has employees or who enters into a contract with a person for them to do work.

What aspects of employment do the 2006 Regulations cover?

The Regulations cover recruitment, terms and conditions, promotions, transfers, dismissals and training. They *do not* cover the provision of goods and services.

- Upper-age limits on unfair dismissal and redundancy are removed.
- There is a national default retirement age of 65, making compulsory retirement below 65 unlawful unless objectively justified.
- Employees have the right to request to work beyond 65 or any other retirement age set by the company. The employer has a duty to consider such requests.

Employers could be responsible for the acts of employees who discriminate on grounds of age. This makes it important to train staff about the Regulations.

Lawful discrimination

There are limited circumstances when it is lawful to treat people differently because of their age. It is not unlawful to discriminate on the grounds of age if:

- there is an *objective justification* for treating people differently – for example, it might be necessary to fix a maximum age for the recruitment or promotion of employees (this maximum age might reflect the training requirements of the post or the need for a reasonable period of employment before retirement);
- where a person is older than, or within six months of, the employer's normal retirement age, or 65 if the employer doesn't

have one, there is a specific exemption allowing employers to refuse to recruit that person;

- the discrimination is covered by one of the *exceptions* or *exemptions* given in the regulations – for example, pay related to the National Minimum Wage;
- there is a *genuine occupational requirement* (GOR) that a person must be of a certain age – for example, if you are producing a play which has parts for older or younger characters.

The Equality Act 2006

Its main provisions are to:

- establish the Commission for Equality and Human Rights (CEHR) and define its purpose and functions;
- make unlawful discrimination on the grounds of religion or belief in the provision of goods, facilities and services, education, the use and disposal of premises, and the exercise of public functions;
- enable provision to be made for discrimination on the grounds of sexual orientation in the provision of goods, facilities and services, education, the use and disposal of premises and the exercise of public functions; and
- create a duty on public authorities to promote equality of opportunity between women and men ('the gender duty'), and prohibit sex discrimination and harassment in the exercise of public functions.

Commission for Equality and Human Rights

In October 2007 the CEHR will take on the work of the existing equality Commissions (the Equal Opportunities Commission (EOC), the Commission for Racial Equality (CRE), and the Disability Rights Commission (DRC)) and will additionally assume responsibility for promoting equality and combating unlawful discrimination in three new strands, namely sexual orientation, religion or belief, and age. The CEHR will also have responsibility for the promotion of human rights.

Equality and diversity

The CEHR is required to promote understanding of, and encourage good practice in relation to, equality and diversity, promote equality of opportunity, promote awareness and understanding of rights under the equality enactments and to work towards the elimination of unlawful discrimination and harassment, including through using its enforcement powers.

The Commission may promote the favourable treatment of disabled persons in carrying out its equality and diversity duties. This provision ensures the Commission's work is consistent with the requirements of the Disability Discrimination Act 1995.

Human rights

The CEHR is required to promote understanding of the importance of human rights, encourage good practice in relation to human rights, and promote awareness, understanding and protection of human rights. In addition, the CEHR will be required to encourage public authorities to comply with section 6 of the Human Rights Act (HRA) 1998 (c.42), which prohibits them from acting in a way which is incompatible with the Convention rights as defined in section 1 of the HRA.

The latter duty applies only in relation to public authorities. However, in relation to the more general duties under this section, the CEHR will not be limited to dealing with public authorities. It will, for example, also be able to provide encouragement to the voluntary and commercial sectors to adopt appropriate human rights standards as the basis of the relationship with their clients and customers in the provision of their services.

Groups

The CEHR has a duty to promote good relations between members of different groups, within different groups, and between members of different groups and wider society. It is also required to work towards eliminating prejudice against members of groups and enabling members of groups to participate in society, for example by challenging racism in the media, or enabling disabled people to become involved in civic activities.

Groups are defined as people who share one of the attributes – age, disability, gender etc. They also include smaller groups who may share an attribute in addition to the one by which that group is defined, such as Muslim women, or Black and minority ethnic lesbians and gay men, or young disabled people.

Groups may or may not consider themselves to be 'communities'. The Commission's work with groups can apply to communities as well as groups.

The CEHR should have particular regard to the need to exercise its powers in relation to groups defined by reference to race, religion or belief and may promote or encourage the favourable treatment of disabled people, to ensure consistency with the general approach of the Disability Discrimination Act.

Northern Ireland

A brief chronology

Northern Ireland has a comprehensive framework of equality and anti-discrimination law which dates back to 1970 when equal pay legislation was first introduced.

- *1970* – the principle of equal pay between women and men is established by the Equal Pay Act.
- *1976* – sex discrimination law is introduced in Northern Ireland and the former Equal Opportunities Commission for Northern Ireland is established.
- *1976* – fair employment legislation, designed to address discrimination in employment on grounds of religion, is introduced and the former Fair Employment Agency (later the Fair Employment Commission) is established.
- *1997* – race relations law is introduced in Northern Ireland (comparable law came into force in Britain 21 years earlier) and the former Commission for Racial Equality Northern Ireland is established.

- *October 1999* – the Equality Commission is established under the Northern Ireland Act 1998. It took over all the powers and functions of the three predecessor Commissions and the Northern Ireland Disability Council. Section 75 of the Northern Ireland Act introduced new duties on public authorities to promote equality of opportunity and good relations on a range of grounds.
- *April 2000* – there are new responsibilities, powers and functions for the Equality Commission in relation to disability discrimination.
- *December 2003* – legislation outlawing discrimination on grounds of sexual orientation in employment and vocational training is introduced to meet the requirements of the European Framework Employment Directive. This Directive also led to significant changes to the existing employment provisions of race, sex and religious discrimination law in Northern Ireland.
- *October 2004* – significant changes are made to employment provisions of the Disability Discrimination Act, including removal of small-employer exemption. New access duties are introduced for service providers.
- *September 2005* – the Disability Discrimination Act is extended to education through the Special Educational Needs and Disability Order (SENDO). SENDO is subsequently amended in September 2006 in relation to further and higher education.
- *October 2006* – Employment Equality (Age) Regulations are introduced, the final step in implementing the Employment Framework Directive.
- *January 2007* – a new disability duty on public authorities and new Regulations make it unlawful to discriminate on grounds of sexual orientation in the provision of goods, facilities and services, education and public functions comes into force. Further changes to disability law are also expected – the definition of disability and extension of protection to people diagnosed with conditions such as cancer, MS, HIV from the point of diagnosis.

Equality Commission for Northern Ireland

The Commission's duties and functions are set out in the legislation for which we have responsibility. General duties include:

- working towards the elimination of discrimination;
- promoting equality of opportunity and encouraging good practice;
- promoting affirmative/positive action;
- promoting good relations between people of different racial groups;
- overseeing the implementation and effectiveness of the statutory duty on public authorities; and
- keeping the relevant legislation under review.

On 1 October 1999 the Commission took over the functions previously exercised by the Commission for Racial Equality for Northern Ireland, the Equal Opportunities Commission for Northern Ireland, the Fair Employment Commission and the Northern Ireland Disability Council.

Since 1999, a number of new pieces of legislation have been introduced. The Commission is now responsible for promoting awareness of and enforcing anti-discrimination law on the following grounds: age, disability, race, sex (including marital status), sexual orientation, religious belief and political opinion.

Epilogue

Late one night in 2002 a 50-something-year-old businessman was to be seen wrestling on the floor in the carriage of a train with a slightly drunk man in his late 20s. During the brawl, the three other people in the carriage did nothing.

The 50-something-year-old businessman was me on my way home from London to Bedford. I have no idea who the young man was.

I boarded the train at Kings Cross as usual and sat in my favourite seat in the small 12-seater carriage. Ten minutes or so into the journey a young man, drinking a can of beer and appearing slightly drunk, got into the carriage and sat at the next table in front of me, facing the same direction as me. Apart from us, there were three other people in the carriage.

Now, almost as soon as the train pulled out of the station he began to turn around and stare and sneer at me. He did this every two or three minutes for about ten minutes. He then began to make loud remarks about niggers and coons and black this and that. After each barrage of abuse he would turn to me and say, 'Who do you think you're looking at?' (Though he wasn't quite so polite; this is a shortened and somewhat edited version of his actual words.)

I said nothing, but I was finding it more and more difficult to keep up even the merest pretence of working at the papers spread out on the table in front of me. I could feel the adrenaline racing. This was pretty remarkable as my adrenaline hadn't had much racing practice for years. I was clearly in the grip of the fight-or-flight syndrome. However, flight was not a viable option. I was on a moving train and in any event my abuser was between me and the door.

To cut a long story short, after one particular loud and aggressive mouthful of racial abuse, he jumped out of his seat and bounded towards me. Not wanting to be caught trapped in my seat, I got up before he reached me. He threw a punch, which I dodged. I then attempted to smother the blows that followed. The whole thing then became a bit of a blur. I have to say that not once did the thought of 'turning the other cheek' enter my head. I remember wrestling with him on the floor. After what seemed like an age, but which was in all probability only a couple of minutes, he struggled to his feet and ran from the train which had now stopped, just as the doors were closing. I'd like to think he ran off because I was proving too tough to handle, but I suspect that he just didn't want to miss his stop.

During the fracas, the other three people did nothing apart from move their feet and briefcases so that they wouldn't be damaged by the fighting. The one woman in the carriage did ask us, in a very quiet voice, to please stop fighting, but the men were mute. After my assailant left the train the four of us sat in silence for the remaining fifteen minutes of the journey to Bedford. There was no enquiry as to my health and no show of sympathy regarding the verbal and physical abuse I had been subjected to. In fact, there was very little evidence that anything untoward had taken place, save for my torn coat and my extremely loud and somewhat accelerated heartbeat.

My story is not unique. Sadly, it is not even particularly extreme. It is, however, an example of the abuse and negative treatment that Britain's visible minorities are subjected to every single day. Most of the abuse does not get physical, but, like my example, almost all of it takes place in front of other people – people who do and say nothing, people who 'pass by on the other side'.

> 'A man was going down the road from Jerusalem to Jericho, and he fell among robbers, who stripped him and beat him, and departed leaving him half dead. Now by chance a priest was going down that road; and when he saw him he passed by on the other side. So likewise a Levite, when he came to the place and saw him, passed by on the other side. But a Samaritan, as he journeyed, came to where he was; and when he saw him, he had compassion and went to him and bound up his wounds, pouring on oil and wine; then set him on his own beast and brought him to an inn, and

> took care of him . . .' Jesus then asked, 'Which of these three, do you think, proved neighbour to the man who fell among the robbers?' He said, 'The one who showed mercy on him.' And Jesus said to him, 'Go and do likewise.' (Luke 10.31–37)

I suspect that we have all passed by on the other side. We pass by with rational reasons: we don't want to interfere; it's not our business; it would only make matters worse.

When we witness negative treatment or hear demeaning comments from a friend or a relative, we tell ourselves: they don't mean any harm; it's just their way; they're too old to change now; if I say anything it will harm my relationship with her or him. There are probably times when we don't even notice the negative treatment or demeaning comments – when the minority ethnic man or woman laughs at the racist joke or comment, we don't always notice that they have been demeaned. We assume it must be OK because they're laughing too. But what else can they do if they want to be accepted.

When we are part of a conversation at work or in church in which it is said that a minority ethnic colleague won't be asked to do something because 'we all know that *they* don't or won't or can't do that, don't we', we don't always notice that we have stereotyped them.

In our many different ways and situations, we pass by on the other side of the road.

It is said that all it needs for evil to flourish is for good people to remain silent.

Our churches are full of the silent majority. The silent majority is anxious not to spoil their relationships with others in the fellowship, no matter what those others think or say about minority ethnic people or others on the margins of the fellowship. The silent majority 'respects' the views of the other members of the fellowship, no matter how prejudiced and misguided those views might be. The silent majority don't want to make a fuss.

Rarely do we consciously perpetrate the negative treatment or abuse experienced by minority ethnic people. Sometimes we don't notice the negative treatment or abuse. Often we fail to challenge the negative treatment and abuse that we do notice. We pass by on the other side.

The Bible commands us to love our neighbour as much as we love ourselves and it is made very clear in the parable of the good Samaritan just who is our neighbour.

If the Church and its members are to make a difference in the struggle to bring about a more racially just society, then we must attend to the three Rs of recognition, repentance and reconciliation.

The experience of many black, Asian and other minority ethnic people in the UK is that this particular part of the earth is not theirs to enjoy, so much so that we have anti-discrimination laws. The fact that we have this legislation is a clear recognition that particular groups of people are treated sufficiently badly that they require formal legal protection. The need for laws of this nature goes right back to Old Testament times: 'Do not take advantage of foreigners in your land; do not wrong them. They must be treated like any other citizen; love them as yourself' (Lev. 19.33–34).

Recognition and acknowledgement of the fact that in our society negative treatment and abuse is experienced by minority ethnic people is a vital step if the Church through its individual members is to make a difference.

I am certain that the vast majority of church members have not physically or verbally abused anyone because of their ethnic origin. I am equally certain, however, that we have all stereotyped people or made assumptions about them based on their colour or nationality or accent or ethnic background or because they were an asylum-seeker or refugee. And let's be clear about the fact that the capacity to engage in stereotyping or pre-judgements is not limited to the majority white community.

What assumptions have you made and what do you believe about refugees, asylum-seekers, Bangladeshi women, African men, Shiite Muslims? How do we come to have these views? How many people of a different ethnic background, culture or colour do you actually know and socialize with? A YouGov survey for the Commission for Racial Equality, published in July 2004, found that more than 90 per cent of white people in the

UK reported that they had few or no friends of minority ethnic origin. On the other hand nearly half of the minority ethnic people surveyed reported that all or nearly all of their friends were white. When it comes to ethnicity and culture, it is clear that we are dealing with differences of which the vast majority of people in the UK have no first-hand experience.

Most organizations in the UK, including the churches, have systematically failed to include and involve ethnic and cultural minorities in leadership roles. This failure is due to a number of things. One major reason is the beliefs that many of us hold about the abilities, potential and commitments of ethnic and cultural minorities. If we were to monitor how frequently we make false assumptions and pre-judgements about people who are different from us, we might find it necessary to repent and review our thinking.

Matthew 5 says:

> 'If you enter your place of worship and, about to make an offering, you suddenly remember a grudge a friend has against you, abandon your offering, leave immediately, go to this friend and make things right. Then, and only then, come back and work things out with God.'

How much more important must it be for us to 'make things right' with minority ethnic people whom we stereotype or fail to see as equal because of their ethnic or cultural differences – to repent of racism and be reconciled with one another.

When black and Asian people demonstrate high levels of competence and ability they are frequently perceived, and encouraged to see themselves as, a member of the majority ethnic community. We can easily be guilty of thinking of people as 'honorary whites'. Like thousands of other minority ethnic people I have been told countless times that 'you're not like the others', 'you're like us', 'we don't notice your colour'. Being told that your colour is not noticed is particularly difficult to deal with. It's as though people can only see you as valuable if they see you as they see themselves, if they make you like them. In effect they need to colonize you.

Failing to acknowledge and celebrate ethnic and cultural differences when minority ethnic people do well is a way, often an unconscious way, of reinforcing the false idea that we must somehow all be the same if we are to have value.

Valuing diversity is not about trendy twenty-first-century political correctness. Diversity is a biological, biblical and theological requirement – it is God's intention for us. We mustn't strive to become, or make others into, clones; our difference adds value.

> Your body has many parts – limbs, organs, cells – but no matter how many parts you can name, you're still one body. If one part flourishes, every other part enters into the exuberance.
>
> (1 Cor. 12.12, 16, Message)

It is time to recommit ourselves to recognize and celebrate our diversity and acknowledge and be exuberant about the fact that we are part of the same body; all members of the same race – the human race.

Appendix 1
Race Equality Councils

Valleys Racial Equality Council
Venture House
Navigation Park
Abercynon CF37 2BN
Tel: 01443 742704

Grampian Racial Equality Council
168 Market Street
Aberdeen AB11 5PP
Tel: 01224 595505

Tameside Racial Equality Council Ltd, operating as Equality and Diversity Centre of Excellence
20 Warrington Street
Ashton-under-Lyne OL6 6AS
Tel: 0161 343 3399

Aylesbury Vale Racial Equality Council
c/o Bucks County Council
Old County Hall
Aylesbury HP20 1UA
Tel: 01296 425334

Barking & Dagenham Racial Equality Council
18 North Street
Barking IG11 8AW
Tel: 0208 594 2773

Bedford Racial Equality Council
36 Mill Street
Bedford MK40 3HD
Tel: 01234 350459

Bexley Racial Equality Council
Library Building
Walnut Tree Road
Erith
Bexley DA8 1RA
Tel: 01322 340316

Race Equality West Midlands
IBIC
Unit 10 Holt Court
Jennens Road
Aston Science Park
Birmingham B7 4EJ
Tel: 0121 250 3859

Blackburn with Darwen Racial Equality Council
St John's Centre
1 Victoria Street
Blackburn BB1 6DW
Tel: 01254 261924

Bolton Racial Equality Council
Office Unit 4
Bolton Market
Ashburner Street
Bolton BL1 1TQ
Tel: 01204 331002

Dorset Racial Equality Council
Suite 3, Floor 4
Richmond House
33 Richmond Hill
Bournemouth BH2 6EQ
Tel: 01202 553003

Bristol Racial Equality Council
Colston House
Colston Street
Bristol BS1 5AQ
Tel: 0117 929 7899

Bromley Racial Equality Council
176 High Street
Penge
Bromley SE20 7QB
Tel: 0208 776 8838

Wycombe Race Equality Council
272 Desborough Road
High Wycombe
Buckinghamshire HP11 2QR
Tel: 01494 527616

East Staffs Racial Equality Council
Voluntary Services Centre
Union Street
Burton-upon-Trent DE14 1AA
Tel: 01283 510456

Bury Metro Racial Equality Council
Oddfellows House
94 Manchester Road
Bury BL9 0TH
Tel: 0161 761 4533

Race Equality First
The Friary Centre
The Friary
Cardiff CF10 3FA
Tel: 029 2022 4097

Cardiff Race Equality First
The Friary Centre
The Friary
Cardiff CF10 3FA
Tel: 029 2022 4097

Chiltern Racial Equality Council
White Hill Centre
White Hill
Chesham HP5 1AG
Tel: 01494 786398

Cheshire, Halton & Warrington Racial Equality Council
2 Hunters Walk
Canal Street
Chester CH1 4EB
Tel: 01244 400730

Racial Equality Partnership Croydon
4th Floor, Oakley House
1A Katharine Street
Croydon CR0 1NX
Tel: 0208 688 8122

Racial Equality Partnership Croydon
4th Floor, Oakley House
1A Katharine Street
Croydon CR0 1NX
Tel: 0208 688 8122

Redbridge Racial Equality Council
Methodist Church
Ilford Lane
Ilford
Dagenham & Redbridge IG1 2JZ
Tel: 0208 514 0688

Darlington & Durham County Racial Equality Council
CVS Building
Church Rown
Darlington DL1 5QD
Tel: 01325 283900

Derby Racial Equality Council
31 Normanton Road
Derby DE1 2GJ
Tel: 01332 372428

Doncaster Racial Equality Council
1 Chequer Road
Doncaster DN1 2AA
Tel: 01302 730391

Dudley Racial Equality Council
16a Stone Street
Dudley DY1 1NS
Tel: 01384 456166

Ealing Racial Equality Council
The Stables Block
Longfield Avenue
Ealing W5 2UQ
Tel: 0208 579 3861

Edinburgh & Lothians Racial Equality Council
14 Forth Street
Edinburgh EH1 3LH
Tel: 0131 556 0441

Enfield Racial Equality Council
Community House
311 Fore Street
Edmonton
Enfield N9 0PZ
Tel: 0208 373 6271

Devon Racial Equality Council
15 York Road
Exeter EX4 6BA
Tel: 01392 422566

Central Scotland Racial Equality Council
Community Education Centre
Park Street
Falkirk FK1 1RE
Tel: 01324 610950

Medway Racial Equality Council
Medway Racial Equality Council
Municipal Buildings
Canterbury Street
Gillingham ME7 5LA
Tel: 01634 333880

West of Scotland Racial Equality Council
Napiershall Street Centre
39 Napiershall Street
Glasgow G20 6EZ
Tel: 0141 337 6626

Gloucestershire Racial Equality Council
15 Brunswick Road
Gloucester GL1 1HG
Tel: 01452 301290

Haringey Racial Equality Council
14 Turnpike Lane
Haringey
Haringey N8 0PT
Tel: 0208 889 6871

Harrow Racial Equality Council
Exchequer Building
Civic Centre
Station Road
Harrow HA1 2UT
Tel: 0208 427 6504

Hillingdon Racial Equality Council
18–20 East Avenue
Hayes
Hillingdon UB3 2HP
Tel: 0208 848 1380

Hounslow Racial Equality Council
The Advice Centre
45 Treaty Centre
Hounslow TW3 1ES
Tel: 0208 583 2525

Kirklees Racial Equality Council
4th Floor, Pearl Assurance House
10–18 John William Street
Huddersfield HD1 1BA
Tel: 01484 540225

Ipswich & Suffolk Council for Racial Equality
46a St Matthew's Street
Ipswich IP1 3EP
Tel: 01473 408111

North West Kent Racial Equality Council
Enterprise House
8 Essex Road
Dartford
Kent DA1 2AU
Tel: 01322 287251

Ayrshire Race Equality Partnership
East Ayrshire Council Headquarters
London Road
Kilmarnock KA3 7BU
Tel: 01563 576092

Kingston Racial Equality Council
Wel-Care House
53 Canbury Park Road
Kingston-upon-Thames KT2 6LQ
Tel: 0208 547 2332

Leeds Racial Equality Council
Sheepscar House
Sheepscar Street
Leeds LS7 1AD
Tel: 0113 243 8421

Leicester & Leicestershire Racial Equality Council
3rd Floor, Epic House
Lower Hill Street
Leicester LE1 3SH
Tel: 0116 299 9800

Race Equality Action for Lewisham
3rd Floor, Fire Station
249–259 Lewisham High Street
Lewisham SE13 6NH
Tel: 0207 587 2556

Lincolnshire Racial Equality Council
Voluntary Sector Hub
Beaumont Fee
Lincoln LN1 1UW
Tel: 01522 551680

Black & Equality Merseyside (BEM) Network
Unity Youth & Community Centre
49 Dove Street
Toxteth
Liverpool L8 0TU
Tel: 0151 709 5294

Charnwood Racial Equality Council
66 Nottingham Road
Loughborough LE11 1EU
Tel: 01509 261651

Luton Equality Agency
c/o The Equalities Unit, Luton Borough Council
Lower Ground Floor, The Town Hall
Upper George Street
Luton LU1 2BQ
Tel: 01582 452126

Merton Racial Equality Partnership
112 London Road
Morden
Merton SM4 5AX
Tel: 0208 544 1333

Milton Keynes Racial Equality Council
Acorn House
377 Midsummer Boulevard
Milton Keynes MK9 3HP
Tel: 01908 606828/01908 606224

Race Equality in Newham
478 Barking Road
Plaistow
Newham E13 8QB
Tel: 0207 473 5349

South East Wales Racial Equality Council
124 Commercial Street
Newport NP20 1LY
Tel: 01633 250006

East Midlands Racial Equality Consortium
c/o CVS
13 Hazelwood Road
Northampton NN18 1HT
Tel: 01332 760214

Norwich & Norfolk Racial Equality Council
North Wing
County Hall
Martineau Lane
Norwich NR1 2DH
Tel: 01603 611604

Nottingham & Nottinghamshire Racial Equality Council
67 Lower Parliament Street
Nottingham NG1 3BB
Tel: 0115 958 6515

Race Equality Sandwell
28 Birmingham Street
Oldbury B69 4DS
Tel: 0121 541 1775

Oldham Race Equality Partnership
1st Floor, A Block, Brunswick House
Union Street
Oldham OL1 1DE
Tel: 0161 621 9690

Oxfordshire Racial Equality Council
The Old Court House
Floyds Row
Oxford OX1 1SS
Tel: 01865 791891

Southwark Race and Equalities Council
3rd Floor, 36a Rye Lane
Peckham SE15 5BS
Tel: 0207 635 8882

Peterborough Racial Equality Council (PREC)
34 Fitzwilliam Street
Peterborough PE1 2RX
Tel: 01733 554630

Plymouth & District Racial Equality Council
3rd Floor, Prideaux Court
Palace Street
Plymouth PL1 2AY
Tel: 01752 224555

Preston & Western Lancashire Racial Equality Council
Town Hall Annexe
Birley St
Preston PR1 2RL
Tel: 01772 906422

Reading Racial Equality Council
2–4 Silver Street
Reading RG1 2ST
Tel: 0118 986 8755

Rochdale Centre of Diversity (formerly Rochdale Racial Equality Council)
Rochdale Centre of Diversity
Deen House
Rochdale OL11 1DS
Tel: 01706 352374

Rotherham Racial Equality Council
Rooms 11–13, Imperial Buildings
Corporation Street
Rotherham S60 1NP
Tel: 01709 373065

Rugby Racial Equality Council
5 Pennington Street
Rugby CV21 2AZ
Tel: 01788 576424

South Humber Racial Equality Council
167 Frodingham Road
Scunthorpe DN15 7NH
Tel: 01724 851811

Sheffield Racial Equality Council
Units 112–114, ACE Centre
120 Wicker
Sheffield S3 8JD
Tel: 0114 272 0012

Slough Racial Equality Council
2nd Floor, Buckingham Court
Buckingham Gardens
Slough SL1 1HP
Tel: 01753 691266

Somerset Racial Equality Council
PO Box 75
Somerton
Somerset TA11 9AR
Tel: 01458 274200

Essex Racial Equality Council
Lower Ground Floor, Civic Centre
Victoria Avenue
Southend-on-Sea SS2 6EP
Tel: 01702 333351

St Albans Council for Racial Equality
St Albans Council for Racial Equality c/o Equalities Officer
St Albans District Council, District Council Offices
Civic Centre
St Peter's Street
St Albans AL1 3JE
Tel: 01727 819321

North Staffordshire Racial Equality Council
Equality House
75–77 Raymond Street
Hanley
Stoke-on-Trent ST1 4DP
Tel: 01782 407930

Sutton Racial Equality Council
2 Grove Cottage
High Street
Carshalton
Sutton SM5 3BB
Tel: 0208 770 6199

Swansea Bay Racial Equality Council
3rd Floor, Grove House
Grove Place
Swansea SA1 5DF
Tel: 01792 457035

Swindon Racial Equality Council
Farringdon House
1 Farringdon Road
Swindon SN1 5AR
Tel: 01793 528545

Telford & Wrekin Race, Equality & Diversity Partnership
c/o Telford & Wrekin Council for Voluntary Service
Meeting Point House
Southwater Square
Telford TF3 4HS
Tel: 01952 291350

Wiltshire Racial Equality Council
Bridge House
Stallard Street
Tonbridge BA14 9AE
Tel: 01225 766439

Council for Racial Equality in Cornwall (CREC)
PO Box 89
Truro TR1 1ZD
Tel: 01637 852410

Waltham Forest Racial Equality Council
Community Place
806 High Road
Leyton
Waltham Forest E10 6AE
Tel: 0208 279 2425

Wandsworth Racial Equality Council
107 Trinity Road
Wandsworth SW17 7SQ
Tel: 020 8682 3201

Warwickshire Race Equality Partnership
c/o Pageant House
Jury Street
Warwick CV34 4EW
Tel: 01926 746811

Watford Racial Equality Council
149 The Parade
Watford WD14 1RH
Tel: 01923 237005

Northamptonshire Racial Equality Council
c/o The Victoria Centre
Palk Road
Wellingborough NN8 1HT
Tel: 01933 278000

Race Equality Partnership Wolverhampton
21 Crane Terrace
Wolverhampton WV6 9LX
Tel: 0151 233 2182

Worcestershire Racial Equality Centre
Queen Elizabeth House
The Trinity
Worcester WR1 2PW
Tel: 01905 292283

York Racial Equality Network
The Gatehouse
49 Cemetery Road
York YO10 5AJ
Tel: 01904 642600

Appendix 2
The Salvation Army's Ethnic/Cultural Diversity Positional Statement

The Salvation Army affirms Christian belief and teaching in upholding the Biblical view that human beings are created by God in his own image,[1] related to him and to each other. It is part of God's creative purpose that we are fulfilled in community, that we value and respect each other. The diversity of the human race is one of God's special gifts to humanity given for our enjoyment and enrichment. God loves and values us, investing each person equally with dignity and worth.[2]

But sin entered our world and the human race is fallen.[3] This has cosmic repercussions: sin causes division, separation, and hostility. However God does not give up on the human race. He has shown his redemptive purpose through the life, teaching, death and resurrection of Jesus Christ. Reconciliation is at the heart of the gospel,[4] so that broken relationships with God and one another can be restored. It affects all aspects of human existence and experience, including ourselves.

In response to the teaching of the gospel, The Salvation Army values ethnic and cultural diversity which it strives to promote. It is committed to upholding and respecting the dignity of each person.

As a Christian church The Salvation Army seeks to empower each person to celebrate their uniqueness in Christ. In its worship and service it is challenged to welcome, embrace and develop the rich variety of experience and gifts which ethnic and cultural diversity brings to the body of Christ. It recognises that when this happens in practice, the worshipping community is enriched, its social endeavour strengthened and the values of the Kingdom of God are demonstrated.

The Salvation Army strongly opposes any attitude or discriminatory practice which denies and repudiates the God-given value of any person. God's creative and redemptive purpose embraces all humanity. Therefore we uphold justice and fairness and will take positive action to combat racism, exploitation, prejudice, oppression or marginalisation.

As an employer, The Salvation Army has in place an equal opportunities policy. It is committed to monitoring the delivery of its services in order to ensure that these are relevant and accessible to the diverse needs of the people it is seeking to reach.

Notes

1 'Then God said, "Let us make man in our image, in our likeness"' (Gen. 1.26, NIV).
2 'God does not show favouritism but accepts men from every nation who fear him and do what is right' (Acts 10.34–35, NIV).
3 'All have sinned and fall short of the glory of God' (Rom. 3.23, NIV).
4 'God . . . reconciled us to himself through Christ and gave us the ministry of reconciliation' (2 Cor. 5.18, NIV).